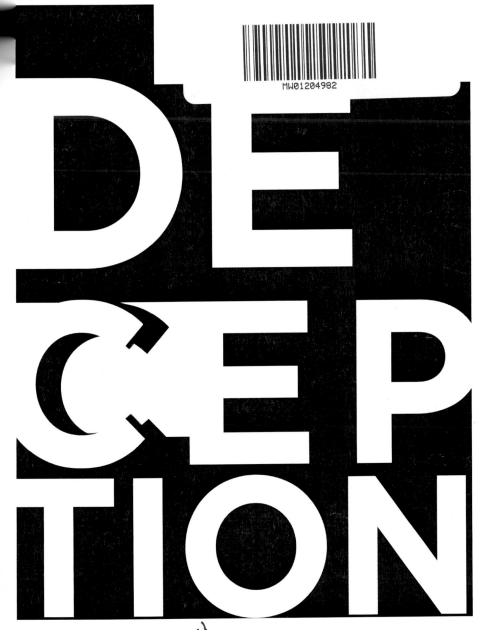

DECEPTION

To Sarah
Best Wishes!
Merry Christmas
Jim Hill
12/14/2015

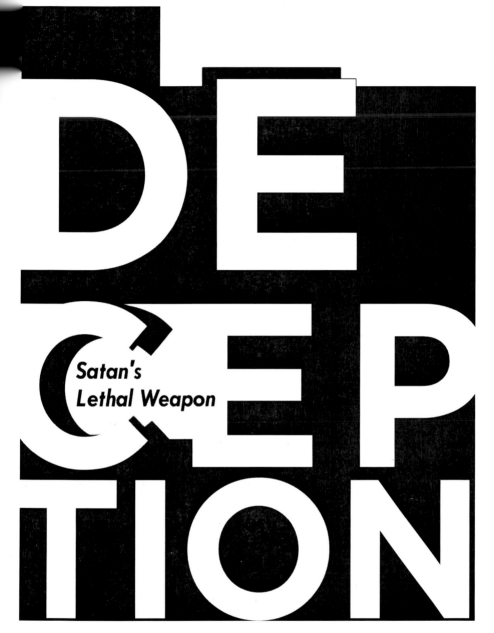

DECEPTION

Satan's Lethal Weapon

Volume 1

Jim Hill & Reba Hargis

TATE PUBLISHING
AND ENTERPRISES, LLC

Published by Tate Publishing & Enterprises, LLC
127 E. Trade Center Terrace | Mustang, Oklahoma 73064 USA
1.888.361.9473 | www.tatepublishing.com

Tate Publishing is committed to excellence in the publishing industry. The company reflects the philosophy established by the founders, based on Psalm 68:11,
"The Lord gave the word and great was the company of those who published it."

Book design copyright © 2015 by Tate Publishing, LLC. All rights reserved.
Cover design by Joseph Emnace
Interior design by Honeylette Pino

Published in the United States of America
ISBN: 978-1-63449-143-3
1. Religion / Christian Life / General
2. Religion / Christian Life / Social Issues
15.02.09

¹¹Behold, the days come, saith the Lord GOD, that I will send a famine in the land, not a famine of bread, nor a thirst for water, but of hearing the words of the LORD.

—Amos 8:11

These days are *now* upon us!

Highway of Life®, Inc.
P.O. Box 1168
Gilmer, Tx 75644
www.highwayoflife.org
jimandrebs@gmail.com

Highway of Life®, Inc.
www.highwayoflife.org

CONTENTS

8

9

10

11

12

PREFACE

[25]And there are also many other things which Jesus did,
the which, if they should be written every one, I suppose
that even the world itself could not contain the books
that should be written. Amen.

—John 21:25

There are many ways to steal.
There are many ways to cause confusion.
There are many ways to cause deception.
Satan is a thief; he will steal your soul if you allow it. Will you?
Satan is the master of confusion. Are you confused?
Satan is the king of deception. Are you deceived?
You and only you can answer these questions.
So let's get started.

Satan continually creates a stumbling block to God's beautiful plan of salvation, and many well-meaning people fall into his pit of lies totally unaware without even knowing it. Satan has a huge web of lies and deception in which to snare you. Beware! Do not be tempted.

False teachings by lying preachers are a megaproblem in this world today where most preachers are truly ignorant (which is shameful). This book will reveal to you the *true* teachings of our Lord and Savior in the hopes that you, the reader, will be greatly informed by gaining the absolute truths written directly to us from God Himself.

You may very well be surprised to learn that you have been lied to by listening to vain teachings of man's imaginations and of man's "traditions."

I write *truth* with no consideration for political correctness. God hates political correctness, and God hates Satan, the father of political correctness.

The time has come for people to learn whether or not they are being deceived concerning the *real truth* of God's Word, which will determine the ultimate demise of one's very own soul.

Warning: Never read or listen to nonsense. Check out everything that you are being taught within your church to make real certain that you are not being deceived! Satan is the master of deception and he's *excellent* at his job!

1

MY THOUGHTS

Our country needs a good cleansing. Cleansing of what? Of radicals!

The radicals in this country need to be shipped out of here at once.

They need to take their ignorant beliefs elsewhere, anywhere but here.

Religious liberty has crossed the threshold of common sense.

Why, in God's name, would we want to harbor people that would love to kill us all? If God was in the White House, do you think He'd put up with people like that?

God has told us how to handle situations that has and will arise. The wisdom of God is being ignored by the masses, and the ignorance is getting worse day by day. How do you think God feels about this? To answer, I'll first go over some of these situations and how we handle them versus how God *tells us* to handle them.

1. Murderers (criminal homicide). God says to put them to death immediately when found guilty with the correct

evidence after a fair trial. Send them back to God. He'll handle them.

2. Rapists get the same by God's law.

Do we follow God's instructions concerning these matters? You know we don't. We coddle them instead. We keep them alive for many years through the man-made guise of "protecting their rights." Well upon their conviction of these severe acts of rage, they no longer should have *any* rights.

Through their own actions, they have given up their rights. That's why God says to send these criminals "back to me." He'll take it from there. He's the *real* and final judge!

We call this land a Christian country, but I personally believe that we have drifted so far that there is no hope left, until Christ returns, to set things straight. He did it before, and He has warned us that He'll do it again. You can bank on it.

Many laws here in this country are set not by God's law but by precedent.

We have totally forgotten to include God's laws in the equation of our laws. We totally ignore Him, and that is a very, very, sad state of affairs.

God's Holy Word is falling on deaf ears. (But that's nothing new, is it?) God intended this nation to be the standard of excellence throughout the world, and we are failing at that.

So are we showing God that we are trying our best to please Him? No, of course we aren't. We are doing quite the opposite, and God is not happy even one bit about it.

Look around at what He has given us; a land flowing "with milk and honey," the "breadbasket of the world," and look at how we show God that we appreciate it!

I do not believe that *true* Christians are in abundance here anymore.

By the actions of people, they prove to God that they are *not true Christians.*

People who will *not* stand up in defense of God's laws that are written in God's Words are *not* true Christians. Just because a person *claims* to be a Christian does *not* make him one.

Atheists should have no rights here in America nor should homosexuals!

Left wingers should have no rights here. Why? Because leftists convince people that wrong is right and right is wrong. But that should never be permitted.

Free speech is one of the basic rights of this country, but we have carried it way too far.

We are eliminating God from our schools.

Our justice system—our courts, our judicial systems of the House, the Senate, and executive branch—has crossed the line of common sense. They lie to us daily. They are mostly inept.

You can tell that I am a conservative man, and I will always be one. When Christ told Peter to fish out of the right side of the boat, He wasn't really talking about fishing. The right side (God's side) is the way to go. Everything should be right. Not left. All things should be done right, not wrong!

No *radical* left wingers will ever make it to heaven! Why? Because the radical left wingers err by their actions and beliefs. Nothing erroneous will make it to heaven.

God has no use for anything radical! Especially radical lying preachers!

The danger of listening to lefties is the fact that they can be very convincing (like false preachers) to the unlearned ear. Radical lefties get elected to office by their promise to give the voters a bunch of free handouts!

Do you think that Satan is left leaning or right leaning? He's left of course.

What is his persuasion? He'll tell you that he's of *all* persuasions and make you believe it. He's good at that. He's a great liar.

Like a ship, he leans way, way, way to the left.

So aren't all true political left wingers in the same boat as their captain, the president? Sure they are.

If I could be in power, I would not allow such outlandish opinions to be aired. It is *dangerous thinking* on their part. (Liberalism is a severe problem in our country.) Yes, it's a plague of sorts and should not be tolerated. Why? Because socialism and communism are sure to follow. We are already halfway there. Wake up!

God gave us the very best land on earth and for all the right reasons, and look at us today. It's an excellent and prime example of how mankind goes bad and is getting worse.

Why do you think God destroyed Sodom and Gomorrah?

They were destroyed because they were all a bunch of radical homosexuals.

God will not tolerate such nonsense and sin. And we, as a so-called Christian nation, are tolerating these perverts in our nation. God didn't tolerate them, and He expects the same from us.

Gay rights? Come on now! What example are we setting for our children? What's next? Rapists rights? Thieves rights? Murderers rights?

We have set laws in place to "protect" these mentally ill homosexual nuts? Do you think that God is happy with us for doing that? Why would God want to protect homosexuals? There will be no homosexuals in Heaven, I assure you. I'm not judging. It is just a fact!

Anyone with any sense would know that God is not happy with our tolerance of them. God didn't give us the rights to destroy them, but I'll promise you that He will destroy them in a scheduled time that only He knows.

He sees and hears everything, and I mean *everything*.

My, my, my. How this world—especially our country—has changed in the last fifty years. We've made laws giving children powers that are stronger than ours.

We've made laws so strict that it has become almost illegal to even apply that paddle of correction in fear of going to jail.

Do you understand how silly that sounds?

When we (old people) were growing up, our parents put the fear of that paddle and/or belt in our minds to a point that we really toed the mark, and that was a good thing. The prisons are full of people who were *not* taught that they must toe the mark, to obey the rules of society.

We showed great respect for our elders. We were careful how we talked and how the words we used were always respectable. Haven't you noticed how the kids of today talk to their parents? Absolutely *no* respect!

We were careful how we dressed. We had respect for ourselves.

Look around today. Go to any beach and look. They dress in disgrace. The kids don't even, as a whole, have respect for themselves. Who is at fault here? Of course the parents are. These things occur because people leave God out of the equation of their everyday lives.

Monkey see, monkey do—what a shame. Immorality spreads like wildfire.

If our forefathers could have known how extreme these "rights" would become, they would have written that some rights may need to be earned because if a person's rights go against God's laws, these cease to be a right.

You see, I can say all these things without having to be politically correct. I don't play that game, and neither does our Heavenly Father. God hates political correctness!

He teaches *straight on*, and He does it *boldly* as He has instructed His truly anointed teachers to teach. He says not to be like a reed shaking in the wind, but to be bold and to the point. No "middle of the road" stuff. Let those coals of truth reign and leave all the political correctness stuff to someone else!

We have gone to the extremes by denying and ignoring God and His truthful teachings.

He warned us (this country) by ordering us to *not* borrow money from other countries. Look at our situation today at the mess that we have ourselves in. No way we can *ever* get out of debt to these other countries, but Satan will clean it all up for us. (I'll bet you didn't know that?)

This is one reason people will so easily accept Satan when he returns at the sixth trump claiming to be God. He'll immediately take care of all these debts *and* our personal debts too. He'll wipe them all out. The only requirement is to simply give him your love and loyalty. It is written too in God's Word that the whole world "will whore after him (Satan)." Did you know that? This book will teach you about it straight from God Himself.

A *true Christian* would know that there are two fathers coming: the fake one at the sixth trump and the real one at the seventh trump; but somehow, most people have not been taught that simple and very important truth. (Probably because their "spiritual teacher" doesn't know either. Talk about taking ignorance to the utmost degree!)

God warns us time and again that the *fake* Jesus is coming first, claiming to be the real Jesus. (This is the number one fact that you *must* learn!)

Haven't you read? Here's what God says about this in His Word—the most severe warning ever issued to mankind—in 2 Thessalonians 2:1–12. (I'll help you understand these scriptures as we go along. Never ever forget these verses.)

> [1]Now we beseech you, brethren,[Let's talk seriously] *by* [about] the coming of our Lord [seventh trump] Jesus Christ, and by our gathering together unto him, [Note that Christ is coming *here* to earth, thus negating the false rapture teaching by ignorant preachers. No one is going to fly anywhere, so get that stuff out of your mind. We'll have work to do *here* for our Father. Read Ephesians 6:11.]
>
> [2]That ye be not soon shaken [deceived] in mind, or be troubled, [confused] spirit, nor by word neither by [words

of false teachings] nor by letter as from us, as that the day of Christ is at hand. [What Paul is saying here is that I hope I didn't confuse you by my first letter, 1 Thessalonians.] ³Let no man deceive you by any means: for that day [the day of Christ's return to us on earth at the seventh trump] shall not come, except there come a falling away first, [people falling away from the real truth of God's Word by believing false preachers who deceive you] and that man of sin [Satan] be revealed, the son of perdition; [the great apostasy; where people "think" he's the real Christ because they've never been properly taught. Well, you are being taught now. So, listen up!] ⁴Who [Satan] opposeth and exalteth himself [by claiming to be Christ himself] above all that is called God, or that is worshipped; so that he as God sitteth in the temple of God, shewing himself [claiming to be] that he is God. ⁵Remember ye not, that, when I [Paul the apostle] was yet with you, I told you these things? ⁶And now ye know [what will happen at the sixth trump, Satan's arrival] what withholdeth that he [Satan] might [will] be revealed in his time [the sixth trump and as you know, six comes before seven. It's just simple math.] ⁷For the mystery [the plan God wants us to know] of iniquity [sin and lawlessness] doth already work: [all the confusion of today is working as Satan wants it, and God is allowing it. Why? It's a time of testing people to see who has really done their homework. Quite simple, isn't it?] only he who now letteth will let, [this is setting Satan loose to return to earth. Set loose by Michael, who has been holding him physically. Only Satan's spirit has been allowed, by God, to roam this earth] until he be taken out of the way. ⁸And then shall that Wicked [Satan himself in live and living color] be revealed, [shown to be the fake] whom the Lord shall consume with the spirit of his mouth, [God's truth] and shall destroy with the brightness [Jesus Christ] of his coming: [and at this moment, we are changed back into, in the twinkle of an eye, our angelic bodies. Yep, we have two bodies.] ⁹Even him, [the real Jesus

Christ] whose coming is after the working of Satan with all power and signs and lying wonders, [God allows Satan to have these powers. Why? Because, like I said before, to *test* humanity. To see who utilizes their gift of free will to seek *truth* or believe *lies*.] [10]And with all deceivableness of unrighteousness [evilness] in them that perish; because they received not the love of the truth, [Because of false teachings by false or uneducated preachers teaching "man's traditions" of lies, not truth.] [11]And for this cause God shall send them strong delusion, that they should believe a lie: [If His creation chooses to believe false stuff that includes the rapture stuff, then go ahead. God is saying here, "I'll even *help* you believe all that false stuff, if you're that stupid."] [12]That they all might be damned who believed not the truth, but had pleasure in unrighteousness. [See how important and necessary the truth is?] Your very soul is at stake. That is as serious as it gets!]

This is why true Christianity is a reality, not a religion. (Never ever forget this!) Religions lie, God doesn't. Remember I've told you that God says, "I cannot lie."

Truth should reign supreme, but mankind in all his great wisdom has allowed lies to reign supreme instead. This is just the opposite of God's teachings. Oh, how ignorant we are!

At Christ's return, the Millennium begins. It is a one-thousand-year period of time and is referred to, many times throughout the Bible, as *that day* and as the Lord's Day.

God says: "[8]But, beloved, be not ignorant of this one thing, that one day is with the Lord as a thousand years, and a thousand years as one day" (2 Peter 3:8). Meaning: One day to God is like a thousand years to man. Or you could say, one day in God's time equals a thousand year's in man's time.

But there are even deeper meanings too in that verse. Just give God's time versus man's time the same deeper thought. I can see that our life (in God's time span) here on earth in the flesh is but a flash in the pan of time to God and—*poof*—it's over and done.

I liken our life span as the morning dew. It dissipates quickly! In God's time, we are here for only a couple of hours. Do the math.

But the question remains. How *did* we use our valuable time?

Each and every man will be held accountable for this *gift of time* concerning how we spent it and who considered God's commandments in the equation of their lives.

Only you can answer that question.

This soon-to-be-Millennium is *the Lord's day*, and it will be a time of teaching God's pure *truth* to those who have not had the opportunity to hear it because they have been taught lies. I think, however, that most will stick with the lies that they've heard and believed in. Don't do that; repent and change your thinking or you are hell-bound for sure.

Satan and his spirit will be locked away during this time of teaching so that he cannot interfere with or influence the masses hearing truth for the first time.

But make no mistake, the opportunity to learn can be one's downfall. How could this be?

Well, your first opportunity was to read God's instruction manual that He sent to us. Remember? It's called the Bible, and if you couldn't understand it, he sent teachers, as he promised to do, to help us understand. This book is one example of teaching you truth, not fiction. It's an opportunity for you to learn!

He gave us the gifts of discernment, intuition, and common sense. God expects us to use these gifts that are precious. So did you put them to use? Are you using these gifts to ensure yourself an everlasting life in the upcoming heavenly age? Or did you waste these gifts by not seeking out truth? Were you content with lies and man's false traditions?

Were you too lazy to take the time to learn? Did you even *care* to learn?

Ask yourself: "How prepared am I to answer these questions when I come face-to-face with God at the end of the Millennium, at the Great White Throne Judgment?" Don't be deceived concerning Final Judgment for all *will* stand individually before our Maker. A person better get it right the first time because that judgment will occur only *once*!

Learning true knowledge in God's Word and adhering to it is like a "paid-up insurance policy."

You are assured of a positive judgment. Not a negative one.

God's judgment is always fair. You get what you have coming to you. God will reward you with what you have earned, and, yes, you have to *earn* it. Earning takes *work* on your part. Nothing is free.

This is as serious as it can be. This is *reality at its best or reality at its worst!* God is the ultimate judge. Be prepared. It's Heaven or it's Hell. You have free will to choose your own personal fate.

We are not to judge another person, but we can judge ourselves to see how prepared we are to meet out Heavenly Father.

We are not mind readers concerning other people, but God is. He knows everything about us. There is nothing hidden from God. He's a heart knower, a mind knower. God cannot be conned.

We have two bodies and there are two deaths.

We have the death of the flesh and the death of the soul. We have little power concerning the death of the flesh, but we do have the power over our soul (our real self) to see that it doesn't face death too.

A mortal soul is a soul that is in danger of being snuffed out. An immortal soul sees no death because you have obtained an eternal and everlasting life with our Lord and Savior, Jesus Christ.

You can achieve an immortal soul by simply *applying yourself*, by studying and learning God's Word, and by having the *faith* that it is true.

God's truth will grow in your mind as you begin to learn, and you'll become hungry and thirsty to hear and learn more every single day. When you get to that level of wanting Him 24–7 to lead your life and wrap you in His warm spirit, you will have earned that spiritual key of David.

What is the spiritual key of David and what does having it mean?

It is the key to the confidence of truth that you have achieved by learning *real* truth. (Not from some preacher blowing hot air!) Truth is "locked" into your mind and is safe and immune to listening to nonsense and false teachings. The *truth* is the *key* to your mind (a key to use if you were smart enough) to unlock it, let in truth and truth only so that no more lies can enter because by then you will have "locked in" that wonderful *truth* that God wants us to have and hold forever.

That spiritual key also fits the gates to Heaven spiritually speaking. So strive to earn that key of David.

Then we are locked and loaded and stand ready at attention to do something useful for our Father in Heaven.

He wants you to have that knowledge, but you have free will to deny our Father's word if you choose to. Don't deny God's Word.

God says: "²²And the key of the house of David will I lay upon his shoulder; so he shall open, and none shall shut; and he shall shut, and none shall open" (Isaiah 22:22). "⁷And to the angel of the church in Philadelphia write; These things saith he that is holy, he that is true, he that hath the key of David, he that openeth, and no man shutteth; and shutteth, and no man openeth; ⁸I know thy works: behold, I have set before thee an open door, and no man can shut it: for thou hast a little strength, and hast kept my word, and hast not denied my name" (Revelations 3:7–8).

By seriously studying God's Word and simply but sincerely asking Him to help you understand, you will soon have that key; but without it, I promise you that you are headed in the wrong direction.

So turn around and learn *true* knowledge. Avoid the abundance of lies that are being taught. God says, "⁴He that saith, I know him, and keepeth not his commandments, is a liar, and the truth is not in him" (1 John 2:4).

God teaches boldly. He wants to awaken your mind and tempt you into *truth*, so you best listen up. (Or do you have the sense of a moth and choose to fly into the fire?) Think about it.

I marvel at the stupidity of mankind. Most men don't have a clue about what this flesh age is really all about. If people will faithfully learn and heed God's Word and take it seriously as they should, it would at most please our Heavenly Father. After all, this is what we are here to do. So if you'll actually do it, you'll soon be able to discern truth from lies. Fiction will not get anyone to Heaven. Be very careful concerning *who and what* you listen to. Make sure it's God's Word, not man's imaginations!

Maybe your pastors will go back and study the actual and real truth of God's Word, repent for teaching falsely, change their ways, and teach that truth *straight on* to their members.

But I'm sure that they would not do that; instead they'd rather proclaim that they are right, and someone along the way has deceitfully changed the Bible to fit their own agenda. So that their (false) teachings seem correct and everyone else's is wrong!

Sounds to me like Satan's disciple. How about you? That attitude is exactly why each and every person needs to study and learn for themselves so that they are *absolutely sure* that they are being taught truth instead of "man's traditions" of false teachings.

Like I said before, every person is responsible for the demise of his own soul. What is your fate?

Do what God says and "study to show yourself approved."

I assure you that, as you learn, you'll soon be able to discern if you are being taught correctly. If you find that you are not being taught truth, why would you want to waste your time going to a so-called church like that? Stay away from places like that! It's a negative influence on you.

I think "spiritual psychology" has to be the main taproot of most churches. They get that spiritual feeling going: maybe it's the soft organ music, the pretty choir robes, all the brethren sitting quietly and solemnly to the side, the huge likeness of Jesus

Christ crucifixion with all the candles aglow, the kneeling pad in place for praying, so on and so forth. And that oh-so-holy-feeling begins to engulf you as all the "holy rituals" begin.

You are taught the things that your church leader wants you to hear, read you a few scriptures, say a benediction (that sounds so holy), and you are out the door and on your way never looking back. Sound familiar?

Did you ever ask yourself, "What did I *really* learn today?" Be honest, did you? Or are you fooling yourself? Most people are!

You should ask yourself the same question after every service.

Then you should educate yourself to a point that you can, all by yourself, check your pastor out in God's Word to see if he's teaching the absolute truth or it is only "man's traditions" that you are being fed.

It is very, very important for people to learn the truth—the real and actual truth. It's the only key that will fit Heaven's gates.

Be not deceived. God says to learn the difference between truth and deception.

That "cloak of security" that you are wearing now may turn out to be no cloak of security after all, and your very soul could be at risk of perishing. Do not let that happen! *Understand* the crucial importance of *truth.*

God says that "¹¹When the boughs thereof are withered, they shall be broken off: the women come, and set them on fire: for it is a people of no understanding: therefore he that made them will not have mercy on them, and he that formed them will shew them no favour" (Isaiah 27:11).

A little knowledge can be a very dangerous thing. Most seminary graduates are not taught correctly, and that is a fact. They are taught to never create controversy within their congregation. The entire Bible is about controversy—controversy between God and Satan. People want to hear truth! So, you pastors out there, teach truth! Put all other controversies on the back burner! Put

God and Satan's controversy on the front burner and tell it like it is!

I promise you, if you will obtain the *correct tools* to dig that truth out, you can learn more in a couple of years what these seminary students could learn in a lifetime sitting in class and being taught a bunch of half-truths and malarkey. This is a fact. I know this firsthand. I know that many of the staff at these certain seminaries don't know squat!

Most so-called theologians are *not* theologians at all. They just *think* they are! It is amazing to know how little they *really* know in God's Word, and they call themselves scholars? Oh, come on! They are not scholars, they are simply wannabes!

I'm often asked, "What's your hobby?" And my answer is "Learning God's Word." (The looks I get are humorous. Most often they look at me with a blank face.) I enjoy, on occasion, a round or two of golf and as I observe my pals that I'm playing with, I can see their vast intensity in trying to improve their game to the highest level they can. These guys are so into it that they, as retirees, play almost every day. Some put in six or seven hours each and every day, and most have become pretty good players over the years.

The sad part of it is that their game has become their idols. They *worship* the game.

I so deeply wish that they would put the same effort into learning God's Word; but I learned a long time ago that it is last on their to-do lists. It appears that they couldn't care less, and that's sad.

Since I live near a world-famous bass lake, I've seen the same thing with the bass fishermen. They seem to worship their boats and all the very latest in their rods, reels, lures, and such other things. They idolize this stuff.

This stuff, as I observe, has become idols to them and so it goes with *anything* that takes you away from spending the time necessary to learn all about God's Word. (I'm not saying that you should become some "religious nut," but I am saying that you should put aside a little time each day to study on your own.)

Idol worship is at the highest level that I've ever seen in my lifetime and is getting worse by the day. People won't put God first in their lives (their love for the sport has become *their* "god" and their idol).

God says, in His first commandment to us, in Exodus 20:3, "³Thou shalt have no other gods before me."

God loves us and He expects that love in return.

He does not like to be placed on the back burner.

When God speaks, there can be no debate concerning His Word. God's Word is final! Accept it, and you will receive His blessings plus an everlasting life, which will never ever end. Deny Him, and you lose it all.

Repent to Him right now. Tomorrow could be one day too late. By repenting, and really meaning it, God will erase all the bad stuff written by your name in the Book of Life that our Father keeps. He keeps a record of the deeds of each and every person on the face of this earth both past and present. He misses nothing including your very thoughts. You cannot con God.

Worship God and His holy truth and come out of this life a winner. A *big-time* winner!

Amen.

2

DECEPTION

Are you deceived?

I write truth and not for political correctness. God hates political correction. Why? Because it's deceiving, and God hates deception!

The time has come for all people to learn that they probably are being deceived concerning the real truth of God's Word. Believing the truth or the lies will determine the ultimate demise of your very own souls. We are in our flesh bodies during this second earth age, but for many thousands of years we were in our angelic bodies in the first earth age. At the end of the first earth age, God said to us, "Let us make man in our own image [let us make man look exactly like we look today]," and so began the second earth age that we are living in today. This earth age is coming to an end in this the last generation. God calls it the generation of the fig tree. We will learn all about it later on in this book or the next volume.

As we begin our studies, it is important that you pay close attention to the true facts that will be laid out for you. When I cite a scripture for you, then you will be able to open your King

James Bible and read it for yourself. That makes certain that you aren't being lied to, and you can see for yourself the real truth from our Heavenly Father.

Warning: Never read or listen to nonsense. Check out everything that you are being taught to make real certain that you are *not being deceived!* Deceived people, who *refuse God's truth*, will go to Hell!

Many, if not most, ministers of today should take careful inventory of their teachings to their membership because Judgment begins at the pulpit.

Guess what happens if you teach and practice things that are *not of God*? You'll be held responsible for misleading God's children, and you'll end in Hell right along with your flock!

If that's what you choose, well, have a happy trip!

You and only you control your destiny.

TRUE WISDOM

Wisdom is, and always has been, the cornerstone of life itself. God *is* wisdom and *all* wisdom comes from Him. Without God, we would have *no true wisdom.*

God (wisdom) says in Proverbs 8:4–14, 17, 20–28, 30–36:

> [4]Unto you, O men, I call; and my voice *is* to the sons of man. [5]O ye simple, understand wisdom: and, ye fools, be ye of an understanding heart. [6]Hear; for I will speak of excellent things; and the opening of my lips *shall be* right things. [7]For my mouth shall speak truth; and wickedness *is* an abomination to my lips. [8]All the words of my mouth *are* in righteousness; *there is* nothing forward or perverse in them. [9]They *are* all plain to him that understandeth, and right to them that find knowledge. [10]Receive my instruction, and not silver; and knowledge rather than choice gold. [11]For wisdom *is* better than rubies; and all the things that may be desired are not to be compared to it.

¹²I wisdom dwell with prudence, and find out knowledge of witty inventions. ¹³The fear of the LORD *is* to hate evil: pride, and arrogancy, and the evil way, and the froward mouth, do I hate. ¹⁴Counsel *is* mine, and sound wisdom: I *am* understanding; I have strength. ¹⁵By me kings reign, and princes decree justice. ¹⁶By me princes rule, and nobles, even all the judges of the earth. ¹⁷I love them that love me; and those that seek me early shall find me. ²⁰I lead in the way of righteousness, in the midst of the paths of judgment: ²¹That I may cause those that love me to inherit substance; and I will fill their treasures. ²²The LORD possessed me in the beginning of his way, before his works of old. ²³I was set up from everlasting, from the beginning, or ever the earth was. ²⁴When *there were* no depths, I was brought forth; when *there were* no fountains abounding with water. ²⁵Before the mountains were settled, before the hills was I brought forth: ²⁶While as yet he had not made the earth, nor the fields, nor the highest part of the dust of the world. ²⁷When he prepared the heavens, I *was* there: when he set a compass upon the face of the depth: ²⁸When he established the clouds above: when he strengthened the fountains of the deep: ²⁹Then I was by him, *as* one brought up *with him*: and I was daily *his* delight, rejoicing always before him; ³⁰Rejoicing in the habitable part of his earth; and my delights *were* with the sons of men. ³¹Now therefore hearken unto me, O ye children: for blessed *are they that* keep my ways. ³²Hear instruction, and be wise, and refuse it not. ³³Blessed *is* the man that heareth me, watching daily at my gates, waiting at the posts of my doors. ³⁴For whoso findeth me findeth life, and shall obtain favour of the LORD. ³⁵But he that sinneth against me wrongeth his own soul: all they that hate me love death.

These pages of wisdom should be framed and hang in an area for each and every one to see and read. No author could ever pen any words as beautiful as these.

Thank you, Lord, for being wisdom.

Amen.

TRUST, FAITH, AND BELIEF

Two excellent verses that all people throughout this earth should dwell on daily: "⁷The LORD is good, a strong hold in the day of trouble; and he knoweth them that trust in him" (Nahum 1:7) and "⁵⁰And he said to the woman, Thy faith hath saved thee; go in peace" (Luke 7:50).

Our Father *knows* those that *truly* have *faith* and those that truly *trust* in Him.

The waters of *faith* and *trust* run deep. You absolutely cannot play games with God. He knows your every thought. So, it is impossible to fool God concerning one's *true faith* and *true trust*. Most people will eagerly *claim* their faith and trust in God, but then by their daily activities and deeds, they show otherwise, thus nullifying their claims.

For example:

If you are attending and supporting a church that does not teach you absolute truth set forth by our Heavenly Father, then you are showing Him that you *do not* have the faith that *His* teachings are absolute. You are showing our Father that you have no *trust*; that He only teaches *truth* and *truth* only. He considers that hypocrisy. A hypocrite is a "play actor," and God does not like "play actors" concerning their personal relationships with Him. After all, when all is said and done, He expects us to *prove* to Him through our *thoughts* and *actions*; that the faith and trust that we *claim* to have in Him is pure and sincere.

Our Father in Heaven has given us many promises, but for us to claim these, we must do His commandments. Not claim to do, but *really do*. See the difference?

The most common verse in the Bible that many people can quote is John 3:16, which says "¹⁶For God so loved the world, that he gave his only begotten Son, that whosoever believeth in him should not perish, but have everlasting life."

Did you catch the stipulation in that verse? "That whosoever *believeth*."

So ask yourself these questions:

1. How can I truly *believe* but not have *trust* and *faith* to sincerely follow His teachings as best I can? You *must* have all three. Belief, trust, and faith all go together. They should fit "like a glove" to be a sincere worker for our Father, for He truly is our *rock*. He is a rock that can't be moved!

2. How can I truly learn about God's promises if I'm not being taught truthfully? Answer: Get away from false teachers. Learn to study on your own. You'll begin to learn much quicker than you think and when a scripture pops up that is opposed from what you have been taught at your particular church, then you'll see that somebody doesn't know what they're talking about! That's how I found truth. It'll work for you too!

God said in John 8:31–32, 36, 47, 46, 57:

> [31]Then said Jesus to those Jews which believed on him, If ye continue in my word, *then* are ye my disciples indeed; [32]And ye shall know the truth, and the truth shall make you free. [36]If the Son therefore shall make you free, ye shall be free indeed. [47]He that is of God heareth God's words: ye therefore hear *them* not, because ye are not of God. [36]Which of you convinceth me of sin? And if I say the truth, why do ye not believe me? [51]Verily, verily, I say unto you, If a man keep my saying, he shall never see death.

Wow! What a *promise*!

That *if* word is used again here and is a very important stipulation. We must keep, at all times in these flesh bodies, God's beautiful sayings (teachings) to be able to obtain and earn our reward of an everlasting and unending life. What an ultimate gift! (But you've got to *earn* it by studying to show yourself approved.)

We all recall how we tried to maintain the best grade point average (GPA) that we could attain as serious students. I recall the long nights of study. We all wanted to be able to present that first résumé showing that our diligence put forth and our school records of perfect attendance or near-perfect attendance would cast forth that "excellent light," thus making us the "best choice" for that prospective employer. Many of us have done that, and that is well and good. It's an excellent analogy.

Our Heavenly Father expects the same of us. He wants us to realize that the most important thing concerning this second earth age is for each and every one of us to be prepared to present to Him as good a résumé as possible when He interviews us face-to-face, and He will *most certainly* interview each and every one of us *individually*. Our earthly GPA or perfect credit ratings are worthless at that point.

He already knows our real "résumés" because He is the *true* record-keeper, the *only* true record-keeper. Our deeds that are written by our names will mark our destiny. Repent of *all* of your sins directly to Him. You do not need a "middle man" because he cannot forgive you of anything spiritual.

It is human nature to want to live, not to die, and in most cases, people that are very, very ill will "fight for their lives," simply to live just one more day.

You won't have to "fight" for an unending life with God. His rules are easy to follow, and all that we have to do is to have trust, faith, and belief. If it is sincere, then you've got it made!

So, study!

WHEN IS A CHURCH A CHURCH?

A church is *not* a church if the truth (and only truth) is not taught there. The Bible needs to be taught to people verse by verse and chapter by chapter. A person cannot fully learn God's total message to us in any other way. By doing so, they can call themselves a church but very few *real* churches exist.

To learn these truths, a person needs an excellent teacher, one that has that *special gift* from God. He must possess the ability to search out God's truth and have the charisma to relate God's truth to the people in an interesting fashion so that they'll hunger for more. (This is a very, very rare ability.)

If you have a pastor that can teach his congregation verse by verse and chapter by chapter, you are truly blessed. Very, very few such teachers even exist who can teach using this method. But it is the only way; I repeat, the *only* way to learn God's message to us, His children.

By teaching in this manner, people absorb *the entire* message that God intends for us to learn. This method will expose people to scriptures that they didn't know existed. It is very rare to find a person who has faithfully and diligently sought God's full message to us.

Deception is running rampant through our entire country. People are not only deceived—they are confused and it's no wonder, with all the lies that are being taught today by undereducated screwballs who call themselves "preachers." A little knowledge is a dangerous thing!

One preacher is telling you this and that over here, and another over there is telling people quite the opposite, and along comes another preacher with another theory about whatever. Blah, blah, blah!

Denominations are bad! They always have been. Why? Because the word "denomination" means division. God hates division (it is exactly the problem in today's confused world). Who and what is one to believe?

God dedicated many, many scriptures warning people to be very careful and leary of the things that are taught. If what you are being taught can't be backed up in God's Word, then you can count on it as being a lie. It's just that simple! Man's philosophies don't count. God doesn't like philosophies or theories either. He considers it nonsense.

Lying preachers are as thick as fleas throughout the world, and God expects His people, through discernment and good hard study, to learn *truth*. It's a very serious business. You can easily condemn your own soul to Hell by believing the lies that are thrown at you. Your soul is *everything* (and God owns *all* souls.) Do not fill your brain with nonsense. Follow God's instructions. Listen to Him. I assure you, He hates a preacher that *claims* to be "sent by God." If people would educate themselves in God's Word, you can spot that phony in five minutes (get away from phony would-bes who teach "man's traditions").

When God created us in the flesh, He wanted to be our leader, our king; and if mankind would have accepted Him and granted Him His wish, then today there would be no such thing as a denomination, religions, or phony preachers. Denominational teachings have created a vast amount of stumbling blocks of confusion and deceptive thinking ever since the first denomination hung out its shingle; and that is sad.

The people rejected God (as most do today) and instead wanted a king that they could see with their physical eyes. They didn't utilize the spiritual eyes that God implanted in us at conception. (One must close their physical eyes to open their spiritual eyes, try it!)

People today are neglecting to open and use these spiritual eyes, and by not using them they become clouded over, and the spiritual eye will eventually become totally useless. A person cannot see truth with eyes that are "hazy." They must be wide-open and clear to be able to see truth—God's truth.

God knows whose spiritual eyes are clouded because the rejection of God's Word began way back in time in the Garden of Eden.

God is greatly saddened and disappointed at His children, His own creation. Look around us. Every day mankind slips even farther into condemnation because of spiritual blindness. (I am praying that the information written in this book will help open those spiritual eyes to be able to see *the full truth*.)

God has become grieved. Wouldn't you? It is sad for God to see so many billions of His children continue to go astray. Don't be one of them.

In Genesis 6:5–7 we can read what God says:

> ⁵And GOD saw that the wickedness of man *was* great in the earth, and *that* every imagination of the thoughts of his heart [and is] *was* only evil continually. ⁶And it repented the LORD that he had made man on the earth, and it grieved him at his heart. ⁷And the LORD said, I will destroy man whom I have created from the face of the earth; both man, and beast, and the creeping thing, and the fowls of the air; for it repenteth me that I have made them.

So we can see here that rebellion is nothing new to God. Refusing God and His demands is an everyday thing, even more today than yesterday. Refusing to listen to our Father is the most dangerous thing that mankind can do. But mankind continues to get worse, not better. Mankind has been lulled into stupidity by false teachings, by false preachers, and the people "eat it up." How sad.

It is *so evident* that these false preachers haven't done their homework, and neither has the poor souls that listen to them and partake of and believe their lies and rituals. People are very, very easy to fool. People by nature look for the "easy way."

Let's cite two examples that go against God's Word. Let's take God's food laws. You can go to Leviticus 11 and read them for yourself. Do it now. Do you see the meats that God tells us that are unclean and therefore *not* fit to eat? (Don't eat scavengers, God says.)

False preachers will tell you that the food laws have been done away with, but that is a lie—a destructive lie.

Christ Himself says, "¹⁷Think not that I am come to destroy the law, or the prophets: I am [God] not come to destroy, but to fulfil. ¹⁸For verily [truly] I say unto you, Till heaven and earth pass, one jot or one tittle shall in no wise pass from the law, till all be fulfilled" (Matthew 5:17–18).

The laws have *not* changed concerning God's food laws. Do people follow God's food laws? Very, very few people abide in these laws, and that's a very sad fact. God's food laws are so simple to follow. But people reject them.

Scavengers on the face of the earth are a wonderful gift from God. They clean up the dead carcasses so that diseases won't spread and their poisons are absorbed into that particular scavenger.

Why in the world do people eat scavengers when God tells us, so plainly, *not* to eat them?

"Man's traditions," almost always, will absolutely make God's Word void and empty. How can people slap God in the face? I'd say that is a very dangerous thing to do!

Here is a scenario we've all seen. (It is akin to blasphemy.)

A beautiful table is set, the family gathers at the table, and whoever will pray asks God to bless this food which "we are about to partake of...Amen." Then the head of the family picks up a knife and begins slicing up that "juicy honey-baked ham."

Do you really think God is going to bless that meat? Swine was created to clean up filth. So if you want to go against God's health laws, go for it, but don't ask God to bless it for He will not!

I want to press this point a little further.

Within many of these so-called churches, "members of the flock" gather together for a "church social." The ladies usually prepare and set up everything to be partaken of, and naturally *unclean meats* are carefully prepared for this event. (You people out there know what I'm talking about.) The prayers of blessing are prayed, and the people "dive in." Well, you just gave God a double whammy slap to the face. How stupid so-called Christians are! (I said "so-called" Christians.)

The first slap to God's face is for partaking of unclean food. But to bring it into what is supposed to be a house of worship? Unbelievable!

Don't you know that God does *not* want food socials in His church? Haven't you read?

Let's learn what God has to say on this subject.

God says through Paul (I'll explain the twofold meaning here) in 1 Corinthians 11:16–18, 21–22, 33–34:

> ¹⁶But if any man [anyone] seem to be contentious [to argue or create strife] we have no such custom, neither the churches of God. [He is saying here that when people socialize in God's church, it can be a bad thing, because contention can arise and church is no place for arguing.] ¹⁷Now in this that I declare *unto you* I praise *you* not, that ye come together not for the better, but for the worse. [God is saying that "I'll not praise you in any such activity in "my house" because you have turned "my house of worship" into a restaurant and "I don't like it."] Go socialize elsewhere. ¹⁸For first of all, when ye come together in the church, I hear that there be divisions [clicks and haughty ones, thus creating a division in the church. Sound familiar?] among you; and I partly believe it. ²¹For in eating every one taketh before *other* his own supper: and one is hungry, and another is drunken. [Eating and drinking can get out of hand. If you want to eat and drink, go elsewhere.] ²²What? have ye not houses to eat and to drink in? or despise ye the church of God, and shame them that have not? [With your "clicks" within the church.] What shall I say to you? shall I praise you in this? I praise *you* not. [If you want to socialize, go elsewhere. A true church is to be used for one thing only, and God expects us to use it to learn His word.] ³³Wherefore, my brethren, when ye come together to eat, tarry one for another. [He is saying that communion is the only thing allowed, if you want a true House of God to worship in. Otherwise you are just simply "playing church," which is a condemnation to

God. You people out there who continue to do this are committing blasphemy. Believe it or not, it's true.] [34]And if any man hunger, let him eat at home; that ye come not together unto condemnation. [Condemning yourselves with these social church gatherings.] And the rest will I [Christ] set in order when I come.

So God's question remains: Why will you not obey me? Why will you not believe me and take me seriously when I tell you my laws?

The establishment of a *true house of worship* is indeed rare. If you have one, always follow God's way in keeping *his house* holy. As you can see now, no foolishness or nonsense should ever enter a true house of God.

Keep false teachings by uneducated preachers *out*. Keep God's truth in!

Don't be a fool! Do things in God's way! When you do, then you can become a *true* church instead of a playhouse.

I can just hear you preachers and church members out there scoffing and ridiculing me for writing about these "church socials." But so be it.

If God doesn't like something, you shouldn't either!

There is absolutely *no* room for debate!

God said it and that makes it final! Amen.

Don't blame the messenger.

3

HOMOSEXUALITY AND ATHEISM

God hates perversion! God did not invent perverts, man did.

God works in many ways, and Satan also works in many ways.

Perversion is evil and *no* evil will ever enter Heaven. Evil doers go to Hell! But they *can* go to Heaven if they repent and change their ways. But most perverts will never change. Some people are born worthless. They rebel against God's Word and always will.

To show you how mixed-up and immoral some so-called churches are, they even allow homosexuals to be their pastors! How amazing! A homosexual teaching morality in a so-called church! (Now you can see why I call some churches, "so-called" churches.)

How much lower can mankind stoop?

In this earth age, society is bending to political correctness. They don't want to upset the status quo by making homosexuals and their evil goings on a controversy because they don't want to offend anyone. And they call themselves "a church?" They call themselves Christians? (They are "playing church" and "playing Christian," and that's a fact!)

Political correctness will be dealt a deathly sentence upon Christ's return. To be politically correct does *not* coincide with God's Word as an asset but instead a very, very *huge* liability! (It will be dealt with accordingly by Christ Himself.)

Perversion is running rampant. It's spreading like wildfire and is out of hand, and God is watching. By the way, since I'm not teaching on radio or TV, I can quote God's Word without having to be politically correct; but to a degree, TV teachers and preachers have to walk a much finer line. Why? Well, if the people listening to a certain station complain too much about the content of the message being taught, they then can refuse to sell that ministry any more airtime, thus killing the opportunity for him to continue on. But I can tell it like it is. (God always tells it like it is, like it or lump it!)

If people don't like the *truth*, then they can toss these writings in the trash can. (Nothing more needs to be said.)

What goes around comes around! Most of us all know about the perversion that went on in Sodom and Gomorrah, and what God says in Genesis 18:20–21: "²⁰And the LORD said, Because the cry of Sodom and Gomorrah is great, and because their sin is very grievous; ²¹I will go down now, and see whether they have done altogether according to the cry of it, which is come unto me; and if not, I will know. [God sent two angels down to check out all of the perverse acts that were going on in Sodom. Lot warned these two of all the perverse men and women there and took the two angels inside his house for safety.]"

Further in Genesis 19:4–5, 11, 13–15, we read

> ⁴But before they lay down [Lot, his family, and the two angels] the men of the city, *even* the men [perverts] of Sodom, compassed the house round, both old and young, all the people from every quarter: ⁵And they [the homosexuals] called unto Lot, and said unto him, Where *are* the men which came in to thee this night? bring them out unto us, that we may know them [Know means to

lie with]. [Lot refused to let the men have the angels for their own pleasure, but they wanted to lay with them so badly that they nearly broke the door down trying to get to them. Lot knew the angels were sent by God with a special message, and they also had special God-given powers. They came to warn Lot to take his family and "get a move on" because God was going to destroy the whole city.] ¹¹And they [the two angels] smote the men that *were* at the door of the house with blindness, both small and great: so that they wearied themselves to find the door. ¹³For we will destroy this place, because the cry of them is waxen great before the face of the Lᴏʀᴅ; and the Lᴏʀᴅ hath sent us to destroy it. ¹⁴And Lot went out, and spake unto his sons in law, which married his daughters, and said, Up, get you out of this place; for the Lᴏʀᴅ will destroy this city. But he seemed as one that mocked unto his sons in law. [Lots sons-in-law were perverts too. They chose not to leave Sodom. Maybe they were perverts who didn't believe in God. So, by their own choosing, they ended up being turned to ashes along with all the other homosexuals. Oh, how stupid they were! But God has warned us in advance that He is going to do this again, and He will.] ¹⁵And when the morning arose, then the angels hastened Lot, saying, Arise, take thy wife, and thy two daughters, which are here; lest thou be consumed in the iniquity of the city. [So God destroyed Sodom and Gomorrah by raining fire down upon them until they were totally turned to nothingness. God hates perversion, as you have learned here in His word. Since God is so much against perversion, why does it still continue, even to this day? Because these idiots love nastiness much more than God. They love filthy sex. They love perversion. They eat it up.]

The lust that the homosexuals practice will end with the same outcome. These practices will end up in God's "consuming fire"— God *is* that "consuming fire." These people either don't know this or perhaps they couldn't "care less." I'll bet on the latter. (These nuts are mentally twisted. All homosexual activities are of Satan.)

How can any homosexual call himself a Christian if he does not believe in and practice God's commands? Answer: Impossible. These perverts are *not* of God.

If he denies God's Word, then I'll have to call him an atheist, and God feels the same way concerning atheism. They are also perverted!

So any so-called church that employs a homosexual to lead them, must *not* believe in God's Word either. So, using common sense and discernment, I've got to believe that the whole so-called church is atheistic also! (Birds of a feather stick together!)

Sorry, you cannot "pick and choose" what you want to believe in God's Word. You either believe God's Holy Word in its entirety, or you don't. It's just that simple. If you believe otherwise, then you are a fool, and God doesn't like fools either.

I've heard homosexuals say, "God loves all of His children," and that statement is true. God loves *all* of His creation, but the homosexuals condemn themselves to Hell by their denial of God's wishes and commandments. If you love our Father, tell Him, repent and change your ways. Homosexuals can be forgiven if they mean it.

God made man to fit a woman, not to fit another man.

God made woman to fit a man, not to fit another woman.

God made the two genders to "go forth and multiply."

I've heard men say that as a young man growing up, they felt like a woman "on the inside," and I've heard women claim that they felt like a man was living inside them. To satisfy these feelings, they took on as a sexual partner a person of the same gender. Now in my day, about forty trips to the woodshed would create an excellent attitude adjustment!

These people are mentally ill and should be committed! We should *not* tolerate this stuff in our country; the same for atheists too. "Freedom of speech" has gone too far! This sick ilk will come to an instant end upon Christ's Second Coming. Hang around and watch!

God created us to act in a *natural* manner, and He fully expects us to follow His word. He expects us to set an example for others to see, and He will tolerate nothing less. By the actions of these homosexuals, they are taunting God *and* His word. Blasphemy won't *stand*, and they'll soon see their "fall!"

God's wish is to bestow His blessing on His children. His wish is that *all* will come to repentance. He also knows they won't. He knows many will choose utter destruction rather than an eternal and never-ending life with Him. So be it! We *true* Christians will be ever so happy to see these "sickies" totally turned to ashes along with "their" father, Satan. Good riddance!

Our Father loves purity. He created the Garden of Eden, and it was pure. He created Adam and Eve and they were pure, but along came Satan with his temptations of lust and messed things up. He *knew* (had sex with) Eve (and no doubt other unnatural acts).

I'll bet you've never been taught that truth. People changed the *real truth* as Eve tempted Adam with an apple. Where did mankind dream up such nonsense? (Now run and get your Bible and read it for yourself. Didn't find "apple" did you?) But yet, we teach our children all about "that apple story," and when they grow up, they pass it on to others. And that is another example of phony "man's traditions" that are being taught in these so-called churches of today.

God created all the races, and He looked and found them not only good but *very* good. God created them pure. He did not create them to mix, He doesn't like that. (Actually I feel sorrier for the offspring they bring forth. It seems that they often have a much harder time in life than most children do, and that is a sad reality because it certainly is not the child's fault.)

God didn't create mules either; men did by breeding a horse to an ass.

Only the righteous will make it to Heaven. Righteousness means simply that we are sincerely trying to do the *right thing*. That's all. Homosexuality is *not* the right thing. It is perverting God's natural intent for us to multiply and be fruitful (but not to be fruity!).

If I could have the power, I would like to clean this beautiful house that we call the United States of America of all the lewdness that atheists and homosexuals represent. Enough uninhabited islands exist that could hold them all. By doing this, our children would not be subject to visually see this nasty stuff. I'd treat them like the lepers of old were treated. I'd isolate them. Sounds barbaric? Well it isn't. God will sentence them to a much harsher sentence than isolation. It's called *extinction*! (Stick around and watch. You won't have to wait long.)

I think a person's rights should go just so far, and when you morally cross that line, you lose those rights to live and comingle with the rest of the population. We should *not* have to put up with any faction that soils the minds of our youth. They are very alert to these trends in our society. It's a monkey-see-monkey-do mentality. Each generation gets worse.

The same goes for all you atheists and dopers out there. I don't like the fact that you hate God. You are as much a cancer imposing on society as homosexuals are, and unless you repent and change your stupid and ignorant attitudes and habits, you are all hell-bound. God promises that, and He *keeps* His promises.

Another faction exits here in America, and that is the left wing extremists and crooked lawmakers, and many times they are one and the same. They are attempting, and right now are succeeding, in turning this country into socialism, the sister of communism. This is called *treason* in my way of thinking.

Our country is in really big trouble, and it is our own fault for voting these nuts into office. Treason is a felony, and they should be tried and taken out of society upon conviction. At least they would not be able to spread their socialistic and communistic philosophies in prison (that's where they belong!). Again, free speech has been taken one step too far!

I've been around over seventy years; therefore I've personally witnessed all these things come to pass, and so have many of you. When I was growing up, homosexuals stayed hidden, atheists kept their ideas to themselves, and extreme left wingers were in a minority. Life was good then. You older people out there know that these things are true and correct. The vast majority had excellent morals. Where are the morals of today? Out the window?

The youth had great respect for their elders. Many of us never had to lock our doors. Some of us didn't even *have* a lock on our door. At the time burglary was a very rare crime. Any type of crime was rare. Today, crime is everywhere around every corner. (Our *safety* has also been thrown to the winds.)

We, as a country, have become lax by tolerating these factions of immorality. Even our courts don't want to offend them, so they interpret laws so as to *protect* them from us, *true moral people*. It's a shame, but it's a fact.

By God's teaching, we know for certain that upon His return to us very soon, He'll set things straight, and every one of these misfits will know for sure that there *is* a God, and they'll be judged according to their deeds. (I will say to my Heavenly Father, "Bring it on.")

So what have we learned so far?

Answer:

1. God hates immorality *and* the people who practice and live their lives steeped in it.
2. God hates political correctness.
3. God loves righteousness.
4. God loves repentance.
5. God *will*, very soon, set things straight and it will *not* be a "good day" for the guilty parties that we have discussed.

6. We'll be rid of these diseased and warped-minded screwballs once and for all times. They'll be turned to "ashes from within," along with their father, Satan.

7. They lose. *We* win! With God on our side, we *always* win!

8. These evil factions don't *have* to be eradicated. They can repent of their sins and do a complete turn around and accept the *living and loving Father* ("I am" that "I am") and come into *His* everlasting and unending Heaven that He has prepared for *us* who will accept it.

Why, in God's name, would you refuse God? Do you know that on the first day of the Millennium *every* knee shall bow before God? Every knee! That includes the good and the bad! (It's a fact.) You atheists out there, listen up; you also will bow to our Lord and Savior. As God says in Romans 14:11, "¹¹For it is written, As I live, saith the Lord, every knee shall bow to me, and every tongue shall confess to God" and Isaiah 45:22–23, "²²Look unto me, and be ye saved, all the ends of the earth: for I am God, and there is none else. ²³I have sworn by myself, the word is gone out of my mouth in righteousness, and shall not return, That unto me every knee shall bow, every tongue shall swear."

Our Father hopes that people who are in danger of being blotted out will wake up, repent, and turn to Him; but He also knows that many are too stubborn or that maybe they simply couldn't care less.

In Peter 3:7, 9, God says: "⁷But the heavens and the earth, which are now, by the same word are kept in store, reserved unto fire against the day of judgment and perdition of ungodly men. [perdition means death] ⁹The Lord is not slack concerning his promise, as some men count slackness; but is longsuffering to us–ward, not willing that any should perish, but that all should come to repentance."

Longsuffering means God has a lot of patience; but time is running out, and so is God's patience!

So what about these same-sex marriages? God tells us about their rotten sin and goes further by throwing them in a "grab bag" of many other misfits and dislikes of God.

Have any of us seen anyone who fits into this "grab bag" by their evil deeds?

> [22]Professing themselves to be wise, they became fools, [23]And changed the glory of the uncorruptible God into an image made like to corruptible man, and to birds, and fourfooted beasts, and creeping things. [24]Wherefore God also gave them up to uncleanness through the lusts of their own hearts, to dishonour their own bodies between themselves: [25]Who changed the truth of God into a lie, and worshipped and served the creature more than the Creator, who is blessed for ever. Amen. [26]For this cause God gave them up unto vile affections: for even their women did change the natural use into that which is against nature: [27]And likewise also the men, leaving the natural use of the woman, burned in their lust one toward another; men with men working that which is unseemly, and receiving in themselves that recompence of their error which was meet. [28]And even as they did not like to retain God in their knowledge, God gave them over to a reprobate mind, to do those things which are not convenient; [29]Being filled with all unrighteousness, fornication, wickedness, covetousness, maliciousness; full of envy, murder, debate, deceit, malignity; whisperers, [30]Backbiters, haters of God, despiteful, proud, boasters, inventors of evil things, disobedient to parents, [31]Without understanding, covenantbreakers, without natural affection, implacable, unmerciful: [32]Who knowing the judgment of God, that they which commit such things are worthy of death, not only do the same, but have pleasure in them that do them (Romans 1:22–32).

Our Heavenly Father has stated it better than anyone else could possibly write it.

He leaves *no* room for debate!

Amen.

PERSONAL CREDIBILITY
(PROTECT IT)

One must always protect ones credibility, especially when it comes to setting an example or teaching our Fathers words of wisdom.

In no way should a person locate themselves on some street corner yelling and hollering God's Word. Such doing makes that person look like some kind of nut. It harms more than it helps. God doesn't like it.

We want non-Christians to hear and heed the word of God, and we want them to come to Christ and His saving arms in a more serious manner and in a much more serene atmosphere than some busy street corner or airport.

God would prefer that these non-Christians notice the many blessings that we receive and the confidence we exhibit in our daily lives versus that person who receives no blessings and is wrestling daily with his many seemingly never ending problems. Just by their seeing that there is something better out there, they will seek to become a part of it.

So we must first educate ourselves with God's truth so that when an occasion arises, we can talk with that person one-on-one and share God's wisdom and message in a manner that will please God. This is called *seed planting* and only God can make that seed grow and mature.

It's human nature for people to watch other people. It is one way that we make our everyday decisions in life's journey. If you think about it, one would have to agree.

If we see our neighbors get something new, we may ask him how he likes his new purchase of that particular automobile or lawn mower or that contractor he just hired, and by his answers, a person may (or may not) want to partake of that product too.

The point being is to set the example of how a true Christian operates his life so that a non-Christian will want a taste of the everyday life that we enjoy so much and thank our Father for. (That's being credible.)

We, true Christians, solve our problems in everyday life so much easier because we have that *good spirit* within us, and the non-Christian will notice that *something certain* that is missing in his or her life.

So we must set that example so that it will inspire others to pray for forgiveness of their many sins and ask our Lord and Savior and His Holy Spirit to *enter in* and bless them with *truth* and to help them to have *understanding* of His word to a point that they will know and learn truth from fiction. People, in these last days, are eager to learn truth, not fiction. It is our duty, as true Christians, to pass that truth on.

Passing on fiction (from lying preachers) to the unlearned is a very, very bad thing to do. God expects us to learn and share the truth. If you haven't been taught truth, but instead handed over a bunch of falsehoods, what good can you truly be to that person who really wants to learn? Well actually, if you pass on nonsense to Him, you've hurt Him more than you've helped Him (never do that).

This whole writing is to warn people that the practices of churches today, no doubt, do much more harm than good. I know that you probably don't believe that, but I assure you that this is a true statement. I am very educated in what they are teaching their congregations, and almost always they are not teaching *truth* straight from God's lips Himself. They teach "man's traditions," the very thing that God tells us to avoid.

False preachers have been around since the beginning of this flesh age (and even before,) and the Biblical prophets have warned us about them and the harm they do throughout God's Word.

Lies do not produce salvation! I follow no so-called church religion. Why would I want to waste my time listening to a bunch of hot air and begging for money! How stupid would that be? It's a waste of time.

As a young man, I asked a young wannabe preacher, "What is the topic of your sermon today?" And he said, "Change," and laughingly added, "changing their change and adding it to my 'change'." (So what's new?)

I have never forgotten that—but oh, how true of all "begging preachers!" *Your* change is how the game is played, so you must always attend a church that teaches God's way and His way only. Do not aid and abet a money-begging "church." God says, "Don't do that."

You must be taught book by book in the Bible, from the first verse to the last verse. This is the only way that you can learn the *whole* truth that is so magnificently written. You must be taught line by line, precept by precept, verse by verse, and chapter by chapter.

Is there anyone, especially on television, who reaches the masses and who has the true knowledge to teach this way (the only correct way)? The answer is yes!

The gift that this man had is amazing. His name was Arnold Murray at Shepherd's Chapel Network. His knowledge of God's true word from the manuscripts was astounding, especially for this period of time when confusion is running so rampant and false teachings are spewed out by would-be preachers 24–7. (Dr. Murray went home to our Father on February 12, 2014, but his lectures are still being aired. He was truly blessed.)

I'm a very analytical-thinking man and was partially raised in a good home, but my intuition kicked in and somehow I knew that the "old school" teaching of fire and brimstone, a so-called rapture, and many other false teachings made absolutely no sense. If teachings make no sense, then it must be nonsense. I was given the gift of discernment early in life, and I thank God for it.

Discernment is how a person should judge for himself the things that are being taught today. One must always take the time to verify truth from fiction. It's a requirement of God. So, are *you* being lied to?

When I desire to learn something, I want to be taught by a true scholar. In this case, I found that true scholar. I've tested him out daily for many, many years—nearly as long as he has been teaching on television. (He is right on!)

Arnold Murray did not know I existed and it wasn't important for him to know me. What is important though is that he taught truth, and truth only, and he'd even teach you how to check out and decide for yourself if the things that you are being taught are actually the truth or a bunch of nothingness.

I assure you that he is the *only*, and I mean *only* [one] *true scholar* on the airwaves in recent times. I know of only one or two other true scholars who are alive today, but Arnold Murray was certainly number one in my book. What a *gift* that he received from our Father and an excellent format to go along with.

His mission was to teach the whole Bible as God expects it to be taught, and he personally took no salary for it. He did not seek either fame or fortune. If you want truth and want to learn truth head-on, he is whom you'll find the help in gaining the knowledge that many people are searching for today. (The program will continue to be aired.) It is a one-hour program; thirty minutes for the lecture period and thirty minutes designated to questions and answers, *true* answers that you need to learn direct form God's Word. Do you get answers from your preacher? He probably won't take any questions openly with the congregation. Know why? Because he doesn't know the answers (or probably not well prepared enough to instruct you where to turn to in the Bible to read it for yourself firsthand straight from God's Word).

Put your teacher to the test. You deacons and elders out there, instruct your preacher to open up a time allotment at each service for questions and answers. Do it. This could be a great learning experience for you and your preacher. (I'll bet your preacher won't do it!)

I have serious questions for you deacons and elders out there:

1. Do you know that you need to know as much or even more than the pastor that you bring in to teach your people?
2. How else would you know if he's teaching you truth or just blowing hot air?
3. Are you taking your job seriously? (Do *you* know truth from fiction?)
4. Do you simply want to carry the title as being an "anointed" and "special" member of the congregation? (You need to think about this very seriously, and you ought to pray about this and think about it yet—even more. It's serious business.)

I'm a fairly educated man in God's Word, but I still need to learn more and more. No one man knows everything except our Father. In my lifetime, I have found that most of these so-called deacons and elders do not know jack about God's overall message to mankind and that's a *fact*! And it's a shameful fact. (And they call their building a church?)

These statements, as I say, are not open for debate. Truth is truth and lies are lies!

Amen.

FALSE PREACHERS
(AND THEIR MISLEADING EFFECTS)

False preachers are a superhuge problem in our nation today (and worldwide for that matter).

With all of the hi-tech gadgetry that has come in for use, the liars are coming out of the woodwork by the droves. False preachers (some are even claiming to be prophets themselves) are in great abundance, and with their false "messages from God," they are leading millions of people straight to the gates of Hell, and these deceived souls don't even realize it.

These poor souls it seems will believe anything and everything they hear coming from the lips of these lying preachers. They are a menace to God. Money is their main theme, not God's Word.

False preachers have always been around. Even in the first earth age, Satan was the king of false teachings, and he had millions upon millions of followers just like today. What goes around comes around, I suppose. He has billions of followers now and the count is growing.

I'm amazed at the ignorance of the people. Why will they continue to listen to and support these sorry, lying preachers?

You people out there who send money, aiding and abetting these fake so-called ministries have put yourself in a position about as bad as these false preachers. You are an enabler, thus, a partaker of their evilness.

God has told you *not* to support them. Have you never read God's warning about fake *dreamers*?

Let's learn what God has to say concerning these liars (and to the supporters of them). In Deuteronomy 13:3–5, He says:

> ³Thou shalt not hearken unto the words of that prophet, or that dreamer of dreams: for the Lord your God proveth you, to know whether ye love the Lord your God with all your heart and with all your soul. ⁴Ye shall walk after the Lord your God, and fear [love] him, and keep his commandments, and obey his voice, and ye shall serve him, and cleave unto him. ⁵And that prophet, or that dreamer of dreams, shall be put to death; because he hath spoken to turn *you* away from the Lord your God, which brought you out of the land of Egypt, and redeemed you out of the house of bondage, to thrust thee out of the way which the Lord thy God commanded thee to walk in. So shalt thou put the evil away from the midst of thee.

God is telling you here to get away from these *dreamers* and *lying fakes* and stick with your Creator; don't listen to them. Don't support their evil teachings. Do not give them money.

In 2 John 1:10–11, He warned "[10]If there come any unto you, and bring not this doctrine [doctrine, that is "truth"] receive him not into your house, neither bid him God speed: [11]For he that biddeth him God speed is partaker of his evil deeds."

How could God put it any plainer? Stay away from these so-called churches. And *never* support them. Keep your money in your pocket.

Further in Malachi 1:14, 2:1–2, He says, "[14]But cursed be the deceiver, which hath in his flock a male, and voweth, and sacrificeth unto the Lord a corrupt thing: for I am a great King, saith the LORD of hosts, and my name is dreadful among the heathen. [1]And now, O ye priests [deceiving preachers who are guilty of lying to my people,] this commandment is for you. [2]If ye will not hear, and if ye will not lay it to hear [(to teach my words of truth, God is saying,] to give glory unto my name, saith the LORD of hosts, I will even send a curse upon you, and I will curse your blessings: yea, I have cursed them already, because ye do not lay it to heart."

Christ said to his apostles (concerning people who will *not* listen to *His true word* but rather stick with "man's traditions" in all these so-called religions), "They're too set in their ways. They are too hardheaded, etc."

And finally in Matthew 10:14, He declares, "[14]And whosoever shall not receive you [when you are teaching my words of warnings but reject them instead] nor hear your words, when ye depart out of that house or city, shake off the dust of your feet."

This verse has much wisdom within it. Our Father knows rejection better than anyone. People rejected His words to the point of torturing Him to death. (Can you imagine for a moment your children rejecting you to the point of murder?)

God is saying in these verses to His apostles: "I want you to tell people of my words of truth and wisdom. If they will not accept *my word* (and most won't) as being absolute, then don't waste your time on them. Shake off the dust and keep moving on and don't give it another thought! If they have chosen to believe in a "certain religion" of man's teaching rather than *my* teachings, then they have chosen "their own destiny" and they have that right to do so because I have given each and every one of them *free will* to *choose* me or Satan and his false preachers whom I have *not* sent!"

Let me remind you again: *Christianity is a reality, not a religion.*

Religions can and do get you in over your head by believing their different false doctrines, rules and regulations and laws, their customs that you must follow, and all their "holier than thou baloney" they spew out to people.

True salvation is so simple to a true believer of God's Word. I said *God's* Word, *not man's.* God's Word *is* absolute.

There is no room for debate when a person will not follow God's words of truth.

People's religious affiliations mean absolutely *nothing* to our Father. God hates religions because they create divisions, and divisions create confusion, and God hates confusion because it will get your mind adapted to believe anything.

God knows that most church leaders live in a state of confusion of their own making. In trying to teach truth to their flock, their "church doctrine" pops up and make's God's Word void (empty). When "man's traditions" set in, God's truth goes out the window. It happens every time!

If your so-called church doctrine does not align 100 percent with God's Word then you're being lied to. Do you like being lied to? (It seems to me that people eat these lies up. These so-called faith healers put on quite a comical show!)

Christ says to us all in John 8:45–47, 51: "[45]And because I tell you the truth, ye believe me not. [46]Which of you convinceth me of sin? And if I say the truth, why do ye not believe me? [47]He that is of God heareth God's words: ye therefore hear them not, because ye are not of God. [But rather believe Satan's lies through false doctrines and 'man's traditions.' God put these words to us straight on with no ifs, ands, or buts. He teaches in a way that anyone can understand. Do you understand?] [51]Verily, verily, I say unto you, If a man keep my saying, he shall never see death."

God's sayings are (when they're all said and done) absolutely *all* that matters. He is not interested in what religious affiliation you possess; He desires to hear (although *He already knows*) from your very mouth that you have followed His Holy teachings as best you can. (But if all that you have to confess to Him is that you followed this man's beliefs or that man's beliefs, do you actually think that our Father is going to be the least bit understanding? I assure you that He will be disappointed big time!)

But a "reprieve" of sorts will take place upon Jesus Christ's return at the seventh trump. The Lord's Day will begin, and you'll be taught truth—God's truth—during this time span, the Millennium.

The question is: "You will hear truth, but will you believe it?"

Well, God will know (because only God can read your mind). But the most important question that you must ask yourself is: "Are all the 'traditions of men' so deeply imbedded in my mind that I will *actually* deny Christ? (Thereby adhering to those false doctrines that *I think* are true because they've been beaten into my head since I was a child?)"

This is the reason that I'm trying my very best to warn you that if the "doctrines" does not align 100 percent with God's truths, then you've been listening to some "daydreamer." (A dreamer teaches filthy lies to you, most likely, all your life.)

Don't you have a mind of your own? Can't you tell truth from fiction? Why can't people see, believe, and practice truth?

My heart hurts when I think of the disappointment that our Heavenly Father is enduring this very day. I feel so sorry for His grief because people *will not* listen to Him.

My personal wish for a person who deeply wants "true salvation and wants an everlasting life that is *never-ending*" is to earnestly pray a prayer like this:

"My Dear Heavenly Father, I ask you to help me cleanse my mind of the false traditions of men that I've been taught (and even seen) with my physical eyes and to help me open my spiritual eyes to your truth. I need your help badly, for I know that time is running out for my opportunity to obtain full redemption. I promise, to you Father, that I'll set aside the time, in my daily life, to seek out your word, and I'll do my best to follow your every commandment. I know, Father, that I am a mere mortal, but I ask you for your blessings. I love you Father and I am diligently seeking you. Please pour *your love* back to me, and one more thing, please forgive me for *all* of my previous sins, if it is thy will. I ask in Christ's name, Amen."

I assure you, His answer will be sincere. The words that you pray must be from your very own personal feelings. Do not wait too long to pray your personal prayer to our Heavenly Father. (You should do it soon, but only if you are serious.) Remember, you *cannot* con God.

Your *sincere* prayer will be as "music to His ears." Even the angels will sing!

This flesh age that we are in now is nothing more than a time of testing. Our purpose and responsibility is to educate ourselves by learning God's Word and sincerely accepting and *doing* all of His commandments as best we can.

Having earned our formal educations and our college degree have absolutely *no* bearing on our Father's decision on whether or not you make "the cut." He will base that decision on the sincere importance that *you* have placed *Him* in during this lifetime in the flesh.

Did you place your relationship with God as the *number one* priority in your life? Or was He last on the list? Or was He somewhere in between? Or is He even *on* your list?

Haven't you read His Ten Commandments? If so, you'll see that He has put *Himself* as the *number one* priority for every one to follow. (*If* you want an eternal and never-ending existence, it's your choice!)

God says in Deuteronomy 4:1, 2, 6, 13, 39–40:

> ¹Now therefore hearken, O Israel [that's us] unto the statutes and unto the judgments, which I teach you, for to do them, that ye may live, and go in and possess the land which the LORD God of your fathers giveth you. ²Ye shall not add unto the word which I command you, neither shall ye diminish ought from it [take it seriously, not lightly] that ye may keep the commandments of the LORD your God which I command you. ⁶Keep therefore and do them; for this is your wisdom and your understanding in the sight of the nations, which shall hear all these statutes, and say, Surely this great nation is a wise and understanding people. ¹³And he declared unto you his covenant, which he commanded you to perform, even ten commandments; and he wrote them upon two tables of stone. ³⁹Know therefore this day, and consider it in thine heart [(mind],) that the LORD he is God in heaven above, and upon the earth beneath: there is none else. ⁴⁰Thou shalt keep therefore his statutes, and his commandments, which I command thee this day, that it may go well with thee, and with thy children after thee, and that thou mayest prolong thy days upon the earth, which the LORD thy God giveth thee, for ever.

God loves His children, and He is giving us not only the recipe to a happy life here on earth, in these flesh bodies, but the pathway and formula of the hereafter.

But take note that our Father expects *work* on our part. It is good to *know* His expectations, but if we don't *do* them, these scriptures that I have cited are of no effect, and thus, you may be rendered useless.

Therein lays the major problem with listening to false teachings from lying would-be preachers. They'll tell you, Sunday after Sunday, that all you have to do is "believe" that you are a Christian, and they leave it at that. Then they'll go off on some story about "Aunt Bertha"! (You know what I'm talking about.) They never get around to telling you that a major commandment in God's Word is to *do* it. To *do it* shows our Father that you *truly* believe it. Action is much better than words.

How can we be an excellent servant to God if we don't follow His commandments (as best we can)?

I have known and talked with many pastors in my long lifetime here on earth, and I can tell you that it is a fact that very, very *few* have enough knowledge of God's sacred word to be even up there behind their pulpits. Their *lack* of a true education in God's Word is truly amazing. Why do they call themselves preachers?

As you know, their so-called "beliefs" that they preach will vary from religion to religion. So, what's a person to believe? Who can the people seeking truth truly believe?

Remember this: God is the same yesterday, as He is today, and will be tomorrow. God's Word is true and absolute and always will be. Our Father is our Alpha and our Omega (our first and our last).

So why do preachers preach different messages from religion to religion and from pulpit to pulpit? Because their church hierarchy tells them *what* to teach, and so these so-called preachers are teaching what some man dictates to them because it is written in their "church covenants and bylaws" etc., which in nearly every case, it has become misleading and detrimental to the members of their congregations. Why won't people think for themselves?

They may truly believe that they are doing "the work of the Lord" but they are deceiving these members by preaching deception. Deception *is* of Satan, *not* of God. Deception is, without exception, Satan's most lethal weapon. People need to *know* if indeed they are being misled.

I've given you the list of aids you need to get. These aids will, in short fashion, prove or disprove the doctrines that you are being taught. These aids are essential for you to obtain. They deal only in truth, straight from our Father, and these truths will eliminate any "guessing games" concerning God's Word.

If the things that you are listening to cannot be confirmed by our Living Father, in God's true word, then you are being misled with lies.

Don't be a "zombie." Wake up to *truth*. No pastor can save you, nor can any "church" save you. Each and every person is responsible for his or her own individual destiny while traveling down this "flesh highway of life," and you should never blame anyone but yourself if you end up judged to Hell.

Always be careful concerning who and what you listen to. God warns us over and over again to *not be deceived*.

Christ says, "⁶For many shall come in my name, saying, I am Christ [(claiming to be Christian preachers]); and shall deceive many." (Mark 13:6) and "⁸Beware lest any man spoil you through philosophy and vain deceit, after the tradition of men, after the rudiments [(the bad and false teachings]) of the world, and not after Christ". (Colossians. 2:8).

God has spoken. Are you listening?

A STRANGER IN OUR MIDST?

What is a stranger, and how does it apply to us in our Father's Holy Scripture? You may be surprised!

So let's get started.

In Deuteronomy 17:14–15, God says: "¹⁴When thou art come unto the land which the LORD thy God giveth thee, and shalt possess it, and shalt dwell therein, and shalt say, I will set a king over me, like as all the nations that are about me; [God is talking about *us* here in the United States of America. We are some of the children of Israel, and as direct descendants, this land is the 'promised land.' It's amazing to me that most people do not know their true heritage, and I find that disturbing. It shows their lack of knowledge of God's Word. God is telling us that when we settle here in the country, the 'promise land,' we'll want a leader, like all countries have a king. And in the next verse warns us who *not* to put in office as our leader. I repeat, God warns us who *not* to put in our highest office: the presidency.] [15]Thou shalt in any wise set him king over thee, whom the LORD thy God shall choose: one from among thy brethren shalt thou set king over thee: thou mayest not set a stranger over thee, which is not thy brother. [This verse, from way back in the beginning of my studies, has always perked my interest. After an in-depth research, I have come to *my personal conclusions*. My conclusions are fact, not fiction.]"

You can draw your own conclusion after your own personal studies on this subject. (But you'll reach the same conclusion.)

Now, what constitutes a stranger, and why would God demand us to follow these instructions in verse fifteen? You can go to any dictionary in the marketplace, and you may find more than one definition; or you can obtain a *Smith's Bible Dictionary* as you should do, and you will have a much better overview on this subject. This dictionary will afford you an in-depth, *true Christian* analysis concerning this word: *stranger*.

Here are some excerpts from *Smith's*:

> Stanger:…A person of foreign, i.e., non-Israelis, extraction resident within the limits of the promised land. He was distinct from the proper "foreigner," in as much as the latter still belonged to another country.…The term may be compared with our expression "naturalized foreigner."… were admissible to the right of citizenship under certain conditions. The *stranger* appears to have been eligible to all civil offices, and even that of *king accepted*. In regard to religion, it was *absolutely* necessary that the *stranger* should not infringe any of the fundamental laws of the Israelis state.…and could *not* be regarded as a full citizen.…*the liberal spirit* of the mosaic regulation respecting strangers presents a strong contrast to the rigid exclusiveness of the Jews at the commencement of the *Christian era*.

Now go back and read this stranger definition again.

And dwell on them until you fully understand what is being said. It is excellent information that you need to know. Why? Because you'll discover that God always knows what is best for us, although we might not understand it fully at the time.

We should *always* trust God's leadership, for His is perfect and without flaw. He has His reasons and it is *not* our place nor our right to ever question His demands upon us. Simply accept them.

All of God's reasoning will be revealed to us soon. So, for now, we'll just wait to get those explanations if He so chooses.

This "king" that occupies our highest office, as he likes to portray himself, sporting all of the arrogance that he can muster, should *not* have been elected to that office. Why? Because our Heavenly Father emphatically told us *not* to.

So now, we are reaping what our voters have sown! We are having one scandal after another, lies on top of more lies, major discord, the weakening of our complete defense capabilities, major weakening of our credibility around the word, the weakening of our dollar (both at home as well as worldwide), massive debts, millions of people on food stamps, a huge shortage of decent jobs, skyrocketing oil prices (when they shouldn't be at all), etc., (shall I go on?). I'm sure everybody gets the point! Everything that can possibly go wrong, goes wrong, and that's as it should be when we disobey God our Father.

The point is to always do things in God's way. If we don't, we get curses, not blessings. It's *our* fault, not God's, for *He* is forever faultless! *We* are the ones who messed up.

I have great respect for our branches of government in our wondrous land that God has given us as a special gift.

However, we have many major problems that need to be addressed in the best way through our systematic election process. Vote those socialistic liberals out of office and replace them with *common sense* people now!

We have become a nation of handouts and freebies brought on under the guise of "helping the poor." In most cases, it should be called helping the lazy. Who's at fault for this? The answer is this current administration saying that they inherited the problem. Okay, but the ones who are in office at this time have tripled the problem. You people up there who hold the purse strings need to stop the "funding" and the nonsense health care program! We are *broke*. Can't you lawmakers understand *broke*?

Can anyone simply say, "We can't afford it"?

The powers of a few cause havoc on the many.

Through excessive taxation (as one example) mostly targeting the rich, we are experiencing the blood being drained out of us drop by drop and getting worse by the year. We must put an end to this nonsense! God does not like it, and the people don't like it. *God sees everything*, and that "special payday" is coming shortly for those in power who are putting these burdens on His children. They can *call* themselves Christians but they are not *acting* like Christians. They are not doing the work of Christians! They *are* doing the work of Satan.

Let's take, as an example, the executive branch in our White House. *God watches* the person sitting in that oval office, passing out His edicts almost daily. Do you think God is happy right now? The mess that we are in is, no doubt, God's punishment for us, the people, because we did not do as He commanded us. If we choose *not* to obey, we get no blessings—we get curses.

I would like to see a *true Christian* running our country, and I do not mean a person who *says* he's a Christian; I mean a person who *is* a Christian. I personally don't believe anything—and I mean anything—that comes out of this president's mouth. He is greedy, a liar, haughty, proud and stubborn, and the biggest money-waster of all times; and couple that with egotism, stupid and ignorant decisions, a "childlike attitude of innocence" that portrays a good-ol-boy persona while twisting the knife off in the backs of the people.

Shame on the voters who put this screwball in office!

A *true* Christian would never ever put heavy burdens upon the citizens of this great country because he would have more compassion than others. A *true* Christian president would come up with ways to alleviate the burdens, not add to them. But the people spoke with their votes, and now look at the problems that we have. This beautiful country is in a real big mess, and with this being the last generation, I personally do not believe that we have the time to fix much of anything.

I can and do respect our highest office, but I don't have to like who is sitting in it.

The voters went against God's demand by electing this person, one who can deliver a beautiful and eloquent speech. But guess what? There is a "speech-giver" of speech-givers coming soon. He is none other than Satan himself, and he'll make this idiot who is in office today look like Ned in the *First Reader*!

Satan will show us how a "*real* orator" can deliver a lying speech. (The lack of morals in our country is a very sad fact.)

The people even once elected a dude who had illicit sex in the oval office and has a wife with political ambitions of her own (she's also an idiot) said that she is "standing by my man"! (Wow, talk about morals.)

God told us *not* to put a stranger over us, but we did it anyway, and these voters, our children, and children's children are going to pay a heavy price for their choice of a person to lead them. We are getting what we deserve and, no doubt, there is much more to come. Just wait, you'll see.

There are many believers out there who doubt very, very strongly that this elected guy in our White House is even a legal citizen of our great country. Millions of people are of this mind-set and believe that his birth certificate smells fishy. (If it smells like a fish, then it's a fish.)

Deuteronomy was penned some 3,400 years ago, and God at that time issued this demand upon His people, hoping that they would have enough sense to do as they were told (but most haven't read about his demand in Deuteronomy 17:15).

Do you remember what was quoted in God's Word, in a prior chapter, that if you choose to believe a lie, God says He'll even send you "strong delusions" ("¹¹And for this cause God shall send them strong delusion, that they should believe a lie" [2 Thessalonians 2:11]) to help you believe these lies? Well, God has kept His word as He always does, and just look at all the problems we have by putting a stranger over us. It's pathetic.

The reason and the way that this guy slipped under the wire is not all that hard to figure out. I know that God can use whomever He chooses and whenever He chooses, and it is my belief that God is using this character to show us how easy it is, for a liar, to deceive the people who want to take the easy way to live life. (And this could be true. The people believed his lies, didn't they?) But they have learned that there is *no* easy way, when we go against God. *Nothing* in this world is free, except for salvation! God charges no fees for true salvation, so take Him up on His offer!

This guy is a forerunner and an example of how Satan will deliver his message to the very same people, saying "I've come to rapture you out of here, jump aboard." Billions worldwide will gladly follow Him. As God says over and over: "Haven't you read it is written—and it *is* written—'do not jump aboard!'?"

I believe the guy that the people elected came to office with a hidden agenda, and that agenda is to do as much harm to this country as is humanly possible, and, like Satan, he is doing his job very well! His pals in the House and Senate follow his lead like little puppy dogs!

Yes, in my mind, God sent this guy to spend, spend, spend but not to save, save, save; but the deeper reason that God sent Him was to show us the importance to always follow His holy demands, and that if we don't, He wants us to see the results of our actions, which is pure turmoil. We *are* reaping what we've sown.

God has told us that if we'll truly follow Him, things will be well with you. Again, haven't you read? It is written. (The book, chapter, and the verse are not always shown so that you, the reader, will search it out for yourself. It's not that hard to do.)

It is God's wish that all will come to repentance, but sadly they won't, and it makes God's heart heavy. He loves us dearly, and I can assure you that it *is* against God's will for us to be in this dire condition. He didn't put us here to be pawns for idiots! So why are we? (It seems that mankind will never learn.)

I predict that many hidden secrets and hidden agendas of this administration will come to light written by many authors writing many books, but remember, you heard it *here* first. You'll see.

God truly does work in mysterious ways, and we His children will soon see His rod of correction come down upon all disbelievers, but most of all on the evil and crooked politicians, the crooked judges, the doubters, and all others involved in this conspiracy to put this country into socialism, a sister to communism. This rod of correction *will* happen, that's a given.

Let's pray to God that we will learn the all-important lesson to *never again* elect a stranger to our highest office.

Let us pray this prayer: We ask for you to forgive us, Father, and forever forgive us for transgressing against your Holy word. We pray in your will, and in your name. Amen.

4

THE UNITED STATES OF AMERICA
(ARE WE TRULY A CHRISTIAN NATION?)

I have personally searched all throughout this wonderful nation and have found absolutely no religion or denomination that teaches God's total truth as He has proclaimed it.

I realize that this statement will be scoffed at, but that is okay with me. Go ahead and have your fun! I write truth only, and sometimes truth hurts, but it is healing.

This country, as you well know, was founded in order to have freedom of religion, and that is well and good; but if these religions don't align 100 percent with God's *true* word, do you think God is happy with these erroneous teachings? Of course He isn't. God hates "man's traditions." It is written.

It is true that God has given us the gift of free will, but by using your free will to believe untruths is a sin of all sins. It is akin to slapping God in the face with an open hand and that in itself is a very insulting and unadvisable thing to do. But most people are doing it daily, mostly out of ignorance of God's Word.

God loves His children—all of His children—but he expects us, in turn, to love Him also. We expect our own children to respect and love us in return, don't we? Well, God is no different.

Besides the gift of free will, God has given us the gifts of common sense and discernment, and He expects us to use these gifts in a positive manner.

As an example, if you bought your child a new high-powered sports car, you'd expect him or her to discern that the car is indeed powerful, and you'd want him or her to use common sense while operating it.

God is no different when it comes to His Holy Word. You should be able to discern the truth of God's Word and put to use your common sense to seek out the *true* interpretations of the things that you are being taught. A person usually can instinctively "smell" a lie. So, always verify the things you are being taught. It is our responsibility to do so, unless you enjoy living in ignorance.

God has promised to send us teachers, and He has. *These teachers are the prophets* and they and their scribes penned the Bible with God's inspiration and leadership.

Jesus said, when He was being asked a certain question, "Haven't you read? For it is written!" Simply search it out by studying God's Word. Seek truth and you'll find it.

A yearning to learn God's truth struck me over fifty years ago, and still each day I learn something new. Most often, it's a deeper spiritual meaning in a particular verse that I had read many, many times, and I thank God for revealing that more profound truth to me. I also yearn to be of a positive use to our Father someday if He sees fit to use me. I want to be a servant to Him in any way that He chooses; I try to learn all of God's truths as possible while in this flesh body.

God says study to show yourself approved. He also says the truth will set you free.

We, as a nation, are in big trouble, and we have only ourselves to blame. We have elected "children" to run our country! The sad part is God told us long ago that in this last generation, people with the minds of children would be put in power, and naturally we did not heed His warnings, and we are paying for it!

We are bordering on treasonous activities and deeds in our country and it is happening right before our very eyes almost daily, yet we continue to allow it. Do you think God is happy? He has told us time and again that if we'd simply follow His word, things would be well with us.

Treason is a serious offense. Look up the word treason and you'll find it to mean: (1) an offense to harm or kill our sovereignty, (2) a violation of allegiance to our country, a betrayal of breach of a trust, (3) to be disloyal to one's country or its' government, (4) to impair the well-being of our government, and (5) to direct unlawfully against our federal laws or authority, the government of our constitution of these United States of America.

Do you notice any of these offenses that are going on in our government today? Do you see any of leaders practicing any of these offenses? Yes, I see these offenses too.

Can't you see that socialism is knocking on our front door right this minute?

Do you see any fiscal responsibility taking place? I don't.

God warned us about borrowing money from other nations, He said not to do it. God said that we can be a lender, but not a borrower!

Here is the scripture in God's own words from Deuteronomy 16:6, "⁶For the LORD thy God blesseth thee, as he promised thee: and thou shalt lend unto many nations, but thou shalt *not* borrow; and thou shalt reign over many nations, but they shall not reign over thee."

Our country is in a dire financial condition because we have not followed God's instructions. (How stupid is that?) The last seven words of this verse tell us why we should never borrow.

Why would we want to put ourselves in a "debtor" position to another nation? Because the people running the show are just plain ignorant! (And most of them call themselves Christians!)

We probably do not realize the political strings pulled by the nations that we owe with our government today. You can bet that it's all hush-hush as many other things that are hidden from us. (I personally never dreamed that I'd live to see such corruption and ineptness in our nation's capital.) We, the people, should be ashamed of ourselves for putting these screwballs in power in the first place! It has turned out to be a much too hefty of a price to pay by the people.

The love for our Father has faded away among our leaders. We can tell by their actions that they do not search for God's advice and wisdom. If they had, we'd never be in the conditions that we find ourselves in today. Stupidity reigns! Ungodliness reigns! Ignorance reigns!

To be successful in business (or even your budget at home) you must always spend less than you take in. That is simply common sense. It doesn't even take a mathematics whiz to figure that out!

But our government doesn't see it that way.

They conduct business backwards by spending much, much, much more than they take in. By doing so, they are impairing the well-being of our government. (That was number four on the list of treasonous actions.) If the well-being of our government is in danger, then it is just a matter of time that this house of cards will fall. This fact is also common sense. Sit back and watch.

If I could run this country, I'd run it the same way I ran my business— successfully by:

a. Shelve all the fancy trappings. Eat at McDonald's!
b. Park *Air Force One* in the hangar and leave it there. We can't afford to operate it and all that goes with it for a while. If other nations' leaders want to meet with us, tell them to come on over. Tell them we can't afford the travel expenses right now. Tell them we're broke! Be honest. (Tell

that other leader, while he's here that he's getting no more checks from us. Tell him that we no longer will try to buy friends.) Stop the pride. Pride was Satan's downfall.

c. Stop unemployment payments. No need to worry about them; they'll make it some way. The recipient won't starve.

d. Stop all pork. Make it a law that any bill presented to Congress has to stand on its own and nothing added.

e. Enact a law making lobbying a crime.

f. Enact the flat tax immediately. Our coffers will grow quickly and it's fair to everyone. We all pay the same. Why should the rich pay more? (That's socialism.)

g. Everyone in both Houses as well as the president should serve their terms for one dollar per year if they have a net worth of at least $1.5 million. Then we can see how many true statesmen we have. This is the price they'll pay for wasting our money.

h. All of Congress will be required to use the same health care standard that all Americans have to live by. We pay, they pay; no more "cushy deals" for them. Let them pay for the mistake they make like we are having to as well. (What's good for the goose is good for the gander.)

i. No more free plane rides for the majority leaders; no more perks of any kind.

j. Dismiss all Internal Revenue Service (IRS) agents and workers except those who audit the corporations or investigate fraud, etc. at the cash registers where the retailer collects the flat tax. (We should eliminate the IRS and let the justice department take over their duties.)

k. Stop the food stamp program and revamp it to assist the disabled and others who are *truly* in need. No more free rides. (Don't worry, they won't starve.)

l. Enact a law that will prevent the bailing out of the too-big-to-fail companies; let them lay where they fall! (There are plenty of deep pockets out there to pick up the pieces.)

    m. Rein in the executive branch spending and staffing. (Much of it is nonsense anyway.) Why does he need a chef? Stop the let-them-eat-cake attitudes. Our presidents are hired to work, not play!

    n. Strip the executive branch of much of its powers. They are being misused big time! We, the people, see it daily.

These fourteen steps will turn this economic problem around at a very fast pace. They all should be given due consideration and then swiftly enacted.

We, most of all, must put God back into every equation and facet of our government and do it quickly!

People are busy taking God *out* of everything, and we are allowing it. (And we call ourselves a Christian nation?) We should be putting God *in* everything, *not out*!

Misfits are a menace in our society and should be treated as such. Freedom of speech is a wonderful right to have in our country but, as with anything else, it has been taken too far! And no consideration should be due to misfits in any way, shape, or form.

We cannot allow any measure of tolerance when it comes to immorality. Our children are watching. Monkey see, monkey do! Good morals are rare. Homosexuality should be a crime. Atheism should also be. Both are rotten nonsense! Do you think God is happy about us allowing these nuts a platform on which to speak out? No, no, no.

God will *not* tolerate such nastiness. God will *not* tolerate acts of removing His holy name to appease the politically correct screwballs and blowhards out there. We need to quickly get back to the Christian principles set forth by our founding fathers.

At Christ's first advent, He came as a lamb to be crucified for our sins so that we could have full repentance upon serious request.

At God's second advent, He is returning with a "rod of iron" and that "cup of wrath," and at that moment, people will feel the painful correction that God Himself will lay down upon *all* the misfits and to those who went along with them. The time of correction is much closer than you think, and this is a warning to the guilty parties.

All of the doubters and so-called atheists, the idol worshipers, the homosexuals, the zealots, the lying preachers, crooked politicians, crooked judges, devil worshipers, and all other evildoers that one can imagine (let's not forget the proud walkers and talkers, "the stiff-necked" and the stubborn). God hates them! (It reminds Him of Satan!) All of these nuts will finally know, by seeing with their very own eyes, that there is, indeed and truthfully, a living and actual God!

God is not a happy camper. Only a fool would want to endure His chastisement.

They *will immediately* cry out with shame and humiliation. They'll turn red with embarrassment, and their voices will tremble with weakness. As it is written.

They'll beg to die, they'll try to hide themselves, and they'll wish mountains to fall upon them. I hope that you believe me as I write these warnings to you. I really and truly do because it is all *absolute truth*. God is the *supreme somebody*, and you won't believe Him either! People need to wake up to reality. Always remember—Christianity is *not* a religion, it's a reality.

Denominationalism and religions are the biggest problems in our world today, and people are deeply confused about what and who they should believe. God says to "follow me." That is simple enough for me to understand. What's to debate? When God says it, that's final and there is no more debate! Nothing more to be said!

No pastor, preacher, or church, or religion can save you, and they are lying to you if they tell you such nonsense. Naturally only *God Himself* can bring salvation.

It is pure ignorance to believe that you can *avoid* being snuffed out by the "consuming fire" (our Father) by simply being of a certain denomination or religion. It is not only silly, but it is the height of ignorance. Never put your soul up for grabs by *any* religion or denomination. They *cannot* save you. *Only* God can.

In Matthew 10:28, God says, "[28]And fear not them which kill the body, but are not able to kill the soul: but rather fear him which is able to destroy both soul and body in hell."

Now listen up. If you choose not to believe in God's total truths but instead put your trust in lies, then God has even more to say to you: "[10]And with all deceivableness of unrighteousness in them that perish; because they received not the love of the truth, that they might be saved. [11]And for this cause God shall send them strong delusion, that they should believe a lie: [12]That they all might be damned who believed not the truth, but had pleasure in unrighteousness" (2 Thessalonians 2:10–12).

God is telling us that if we choose to believe that a particular religion is the only one, then He'll help you out by making you delusional to the point of putting your soul in grave and serious danger of nonexistence. God is trying to wake people up to the *reality and to understand* the purpose of life itself while in these flesh bodies.

God does not want us to fall into deception, Satan's most lethal weapon.

Here is God's wish for all of us as He says, "[11]Put on the whole armour of God, that ye may be able to *stand* against the wiles of the devil" (Ephesians 6:11).

What is this "whole armour?" Well, it is God's total truth, it's *God's Word—not man's word* or false traditions of men.

Did you notice the word *stand* that is italicized? God is telling us here that by learning and trusting in God's Word, we'll have the knowledge and powers to stand against Satan upon his coming at the sixth trump. If we are uneducated in God's Word, what happens then? Well, we *fall!* (See how good our Father is to us by giving us this warning in advance.) God has *kept* His word of truth because He has, indeed, foretold us all things and how to overcome all adversities by putting on God's whole armour.

I suppose the readers of this writing may think that I'm coming across to you a little bit harsh and salty; but God has given us a little view into *His* mind, His thinking.

God says, "³⁴Salt *is* good: but if the salt have lost his savour, wherewith shall it be seasoned?" (Luke 14:34).

God does not like sugarcoated salt. He wants His word to stand out with flavor. So I tell it like it is, and I make no apologies. He never wants His word to be dressed down by sugarcoating it. He wants it taught straight on! (He used an excellent analogy.)

We, as a nation, need to learn all that we possibly can concerning our holy Father's instructions and advice as a blessing to Him for giving us this beautiful and bountiful land that we call the United States. We didn't simply stumble on to this *terra firma*. God is the reason we are here in this location, for He masterminded the plan long ago.

Some people readily admit that they know God and say their prayers to Him every single day, and that is a good thing to do when one is sincere and truly honest with Him. (People cannot con or trick Him in any way, He *knows* your mind. He even knows your every thought!) Sincerity is the key word when dealing with our Heavenly Father.

But in 1 John 2:4–5, God says: "⁴He that saith, I know him, and keepeth not his commandments, is a liar, and the truth is not in him. ⁵But whoso keepeth his word, in him verily [truly] is the love of God perfected [matured]; hereby know we that we are in him."

Many may *say* (in passing) that they love God, but as you can see, there is much more involved than just talk. It takes *action* on our part to mature in living His commandments as best we can.

We don't want to be called liars by God Himself, do we?

God wants us to *prove* our love for Him, and that takes a sincere effort on our part. We must study His word long and hard because God tells us that we *must* study to show ourselves approved. Simply sitting on a pew, listening to some fruitcake blow hot air doesn't get the job done.

So you must ask yourself where do I want to end up? Is it worth the effort? Well, only *you* can answer that.

You cannot proclaim love as true love with words only. God is no fool, you know!

God is our *true* Father. God is our *closest* of kin. Have you ever thought about that? God is *every* person's closest of kin, no matter what race. After creating us, He looked down at us and not only said that it is good but *very* good.

God is no respecter of persons, whether rich or poor, whether you are a man, woman, or child. He gives us, every single entity, the very same opportunities to sincerely prove our true and sincere love for Him. Most people do not realize that this earth age (being the second) was created for *us*, enfleshed men and women.

God has appointed us *one* duty, and it is the *main* duty that He's given us. This ultimate duty is for us to decide between Him and Satan. *This is the ultimate bottom line*. It's all that truly counts to God. It's what life is all about.

If you love God and wish to please Him, you'll dig into His Word and learn! This is our purpose here—our true main purpose. Heaven was created as a reward and a blessing for those who diligently seek it. Nothing is free, you know! Hell was created for those who couldn't care less.

God doesn't care about all the successes you may have had while here in this flesh age. He doesn't care how many academic degrees you have or what offices you've held or the amount of money you've amassed. He only cares about one simple little word: *Love*. You have shown and proved your true *love* for Him or you haven't. There are only two choices. Choose to please God *or* choose to please Satan.

God is on a one-on-one basis with every single person. It's just *you* and *Him*! If you care, talk with Him. He'd love to hear from you!

Whom have you chosen, God or Satan? Judgment will be swift and in many cases, it will be lethal.

Do you truly have salvation or do you just *think* that you are saved?

Do not be deceived by false denominational teaching!

Like I said, God works on a one-on-one basis, and everyone must gain a one-on-one relationship with our maker upstairs, our Heavenly Father.

It's Heaven or Hell. Sorry, there is no in-between!

Amen!

RELIGIONS AND DENOMINATIONS (IGNORANCE RUNS RAMPANT!)

Since the beginning of time people have dreamed up many hundreds, if not thousands, of religions, resulting in the establishing of many, many denominations.

The people shunned our Heavenly Father who wanted to be our spiritual leader and our king; but the people wanted someone who they could see and touch. (Imagine how God felt about that!) Our very creator wasn't good enough for man. They needed some man to listen to and to obey and even worship and to follow his beliefs, not God's truths. Man's lies and vain imaginations have become the norm of today's teachings, and that's sad. (By the way, God is nondenominational.)

I recall, as a lad, that my favorite verse in the King James Version of the Bible was Ephesians 6:11: "Put on the whole armor of God so that ye may be able to *stand* against the wiles of the Devil," and this piqued my interest greatly to learn God's whole word, the letter that he sent us to study, to have, and to understand. (It's God's *word to the wise*, it can be said.)

When I became a young adult, I began my serious studies into the wisdom that He sent to us. I like to call it God's "love letter" to us here in this flesh age. In this letter from our Heavenly

Father, we can obtain unending blessings along with creating a secured eternal life. Or by ignoring God's Word, a quick trip to Hell to be snuffed from existence at the time of the Great White Throne Judgment at the end of the Millennium age. God wants us to please Him by studying His word and to try our best to understand; it gives Him great pleasure to know that we are trying. You can read in Revelations 4:11 where God says that He created everything for His pleasure. (So you must ask yourself, "Have I pleased Him lately?") Give it much serious thought. Your very soul is at stake! We have free will to choose our *own* ultimate demise. Let's give God pleasure, not disappointment.

The Ten Commandments are being flushed down the toilet. The least sign of anything Christian is becoming taboo (and at a very fast pace). How do you think our Father in Heaven is feeling about all this? Do you think that he hates all this mess we've created? (You can be certain he does.) The people that put into law these so-called rules to delete God's name will soon meet God face-to-face and have to answer for their actions. (They will be severely judged.) Give this serious consideration. (Will you be one to say to Him, "God, I don't really care what you think"?) Will you be one day too late to even be granted forgiveness? God is our ultimate judge. Vengeance belongs to Him. (Go to the closet of your mind and give it deep consideration.)

A vast majority of people *claim* to be Christians and that is a good thing, *or* is it?

I have to wonder, again, if most people realize what they are really saying when they make that declaration. Are they truly a Christian or do they just *claim* to be a "Christ man?" I wonder if they know that their every deed—good or bad—is being recorded beside their name in the Book of Life (which will be opened on Judgment Day by our Heavenly Father Himself), and that everyone will come face-to-face with God. How awesome! (Ponder on that awhile. That runs pretty deep, doesn't it?)

Do you *really* believe that it will happen? Have you ever heard of the Great White Throne Judgment? Do you *really* believe your deeds are being recorded, or that He even knows your every thought? Have you ever been taught that He knows and watches everything? Have you ever thought about how you'll answer the questions that He will ask of you when it's your turn to be one-on-one with Him? Have you?

Have you been taught the truth from God's Word? Have you personally ever verified the teachings of your pastor? Do you innocently *believe* everything that you are being taught? Are you being taught lies? How do you actually know if your preacher's message to you is really true? Do you even care? Do you care enough about your very soul to want to guard and feed it with truth only?

Each of these questions needs to be answered. It's a strictly personal thing between you and our Heavenly Father.

Your everlasting being will hang in the balance by what you are being taught. If you've been taught lies and want to be ignorant of truth, well you have free will to do so. But if you want truth and truth only, it will require "work" on your part. You can dig that truth out of God's "Book of instructions" (the Bible) that He sent along for us to learn, and to learn well! There are no free rides! A person must study! Is it *worth* it to you?

Don't be ignorant of God's Word. Ignorant is not a bad word, it simply means that you don't know. If you choose to be ignorant and to simply get your daily so-called truth from a preacher or teacher who *most likely* doesn't know up from down about God's Word, then what have your learned? Following false teachings will *not* get you into Heaven. *Truth* rules.

Do you entrust the demise of your soul to your pastor? Do you entrust your soul to be saved from Hell by believing false teachings? Do you choose to remain ignorant? God hopes not. *But* you *do* have free will.

It's a real shame how people will shrug off real truth from God's Word. I suppose they are happier believing the lies they've been taught throughout their lives, or are they simply too lazy to put forth the effort to learn the truth?

I assure you that when you come face-to-face in a one-on-one meeting with God Himself, you'll wish that His *saving mercy* will fall upon you. But will it? God is the judge, the *only* judge who matters ultimately, and He'll judge you fairly. He'll give everyone exactly what they deserve all at one time! Rewards *can* be good, or rewards can be bad. Each person fully controls his or her rewards when Judgment Day arrives, and it *will* arrive soon.

Look at it this way: If you had a child that never followed your instructions, never told you that he or she loves you, would you think much good of him or her? Wouldn't it hurt and disappoint you? (Sure it would.) Jesus taught truth and nothing but the truth, and what did the people do to Him? They spat upon Him. They taunted Him. They beat Him. They rejected Him. They called Him a liar. And then they killed Him? (I'll bet they called themselves Christians too. Oh, really?)

This book will teach you truth from fiction. It will teach you that judgment begins at the pulpit. I have been around a long time and have learned that most people are being taught lies. Our children are being taught lies (the story in the Garden of Eden and about the apple, the Easter bunny, the so-called rapture, etc). And these little ones grow up and pass these teachings on to the next generation and so on and so forth. They do this out of ignorance. How sad.

In this book, you'll learn the *truth not lies*!

Another statement I'd like to make is this: Almost all so-called denominations (man's religions) and their church leaders teach lies—lie after lie (but they think it's truth). So if you choose to believe lies, this book is not for you. (Or *maybe* you'll find that this book follows God's truth with a capital *T*.) Want to learn? Well, read on!

There are *no* lies being written here, just the simple truth. Christ taught straight-down-the-line truth with no apologies. You can *like* it, or you can *hate* it. It's up to you and you alone. It's totally an individual thing. No preacher or church can save you from Hell. No denomination can save your soul, only God can.

God owns all souls, therefore; He can do whatever He *wishes* with them, and He will. It's a fact!

Do you know God hates the word *denomination*? Know why? Denomination means division. All so-called denominations teach different stuff. You may say how "holy" a church seems or that you received your pep talk for the week, but what did you really learn from *God's Word*? You probably learned very little or nothing at all. Don't fool yourself for the time is approaching very swiftly that you'll be held responsible for your so-called beliefs. Are they all proven facts of *pure truth* from what God says, or is your knowledge gained from what man says. Think about this. Give it deep meditations and do it now, don't wait. Learn truth! It's the *only* thing that can possibly save you.

To learn God's truth (for there is no other), one must flush out his or her mind all of what you think you know and have learned and seek only *truth* from God's word. If you will do this, then you'll learn if you are indeed a *true* Christian, or if you've been misled into believing a bunch of nonsense. You need to know. Heaven is based on truth; Hell is based on nonsense.

The most important thing you must learn is that our Heavenly Father loves us all. He loves all the races. He made us all and gave us two bodies. He gave us this flesh body and put our souls inside it to dwell there until we die and return to Him. He gives us free will to decide what we want to fill our minds with, either good or bad. If we learn good, then on Judgment Day we'll get our just rewards for our good deeds and for searching and feeding those souls with truth, but if our souls are filled with evil and false teachings, we'll get our just rewards for that too. We are judged by our works and deeds while we are here in the flesh. Our works and our deeds are all that we can take with us when we die. Nothing else will go with us. That is what life is really all about. The ultimate outcome of our Heavenly Father's judgment should be our number one priority because it is also *His* number one priority. Nothing else matters. If you follow Satan and his soul-destroying ways, then the *death* of your soul (your soul *is* you) is exactly what you'll reap. You'll be judged to Hell. (Or you can still turn things around and receive God's promises of everlasting life and the beautiful Heaven that we'll dwell in forever and ever. There will be no end. Don't you want to go there? Of course you do; we all do.)

Since we were raised with beginnings and endings, we have tried to understand the word *forever*, and that is quite a task. We have a beginning and an ending to everything we do in these flesh bodies here on earth. Everything starts with a *beginning* and comes to an *end*. But God has created the realm of *forever*. It gets kind of mind-boggling when you think about it deeply. No end—*never* an end.

Wow! Look into space on a clear night, and you'll see *no end*. It's impossible to fathom that there is no end to something. I pray and hope to be a part of *forever*. Don't you too? Sure you do!

It's the easiest thing in this world for you to have your part of *forever*. God loves you and wants you to gain the knowledge of His words of truth and to do your best to always do the right things in life. We *all* mess up from time to time but when we repent to God, and God alone, He'll forgive us. Forgiveness is a beautiful thing. When you ask Him for forgiveness, you are to always deeply *mean* it. You can't trick God. Don't even try it. Simply repent to God and then change your ways. That's what you do, just simply talk to Him. If you have a written prayer that you read to Him, I want you to trash it! God doesn't like it. He knows when you're sincere. How would you like it if your child came up to you, pulled out a piece of paper, and started reading it to you? How sincere is that? Well, God is no different because He sincerely wants you to mean it *from your heart*. He *will* forgive you and erase those sins that were written by your name in the Book of Life, and He will give you that *new start*. How wonderful He is. Repentance is a beautiful gift from God. So use that *gift* daily. But you must mean it; otherwise, don't waste His time! (A lack of sincerity is a sin in and of itself.)

Let's please our Father! Let's *truly* love Him. After all, He *is* our *true* Father. He is the Father of all fathers.

All of you people out there, you are my true brothers and sisters, no matter what your color is. We are *all* equal! Equality reigns with our Father.

Amen.

GOD'S FOOD LAWS
(THE GOOD AND THE BAD)

Swine were created by God to keep disease off of the face of the earth and away from mankind. Hogs are scavengers, and God did not create swine to be eaten by mankind. Don't eat pork! Don't consume any of God's scavengers. It's a sin.

Don't you believe that God knows what He's doing by giving us these food laws?

Do you think that our Father is an idiot?

You'll have these lying preachers and teachers tell you that these laws were done away with in the New Testament. Why (with all their "infinite wisdom") haven't they learned to read? God has *never* changed His food laws.

I know many people who are close to me and around me know that scavengers should not be ingested in our bodies, but they eat it anyway. The food laws should be followed (if for no other reason) to simply please our Father. If people cannot follow these *simple* laws, how can they follow *anything* that God demands of us? (One should really give this strong consideration. It runs deeper than you think!)

Most churches feed their "flock" in their little get-togethers, and these will nearly always include pork and other meats that were *not* created to be partaken of. They ask God to "bless this food" in their orations of prayers. (This is a form of blasphemy.) And they call this a "house of God?" God will not bless food like that. Do you know that a *true church* is not supposed to eat on their church property? The church is for one purpose only, and that is to teach God's Word and nothing else. God says to eat at home or elsewhere but *not in church*!

If you think that God will bless that food, you are sadly mistaken. These so-called church members need to *wake up to truth* and obey God's teachings as best they can because the day will soon come when "every knee shall bow before God Himself and every person will have to give account of himself" to God.

Go to Romans 14:10–12:

> [10]But why dost thou judge thy brother? or why dost thou set at nought thy brother? for we shall all stand before the judgment seat of Christ. [11]For it is written, As I live, saith the Lord, every knee shall bow to me, and every tongue shall confess to God. [12]So then every one of us shall give account of himself to God.

Let those verses stick with you throughout all your life. If you'll do as God says, I do assure you of God's *true blessings*. (Not the blessings that people "think" are coming from God, but God's true blessings that they will *know* is coming from God.) If your church does *not* teach God's Word and God's Word only, then it is not a church that God approves of or will bless. Just hang around and you'll see for yourself that you very well may be attending a church founded by man's traditions and not by God's truths. If you are partaking of man's traditions there, you best run as fast as you can and depart from such foolishness and nonsense. You've been duped! You've been lied to by your preacher and his pure ignorance of God's Word. God tells us that His Word should be taught chapter by chapter, line by line, precept on precept, and that the person teaching you should be educated in God's Word so that he can present those truths in such a way that they can be understood by all. (Sure makes sense to me.) Church is not a playhouse but is a place of the *healing* of the soul, the education of the soul. So you must *not eat* there, you should *not play* there, you should *not listen to mans' traditions* there, and you should never ever listen to lies and nonsense there. Nor should you ever listen to beggars for money there. God doesn't like it one bit! God does not send out beggars. If a preacher or teacher is truly mature in

God's Word, he'll have enough blessings come his way that it won't be necessary for him to continually bring up those special "love offerings" or "building offerings" to add to this or that, etc. If you are asked to sign a pledge, don't do that either. God does not like it. Why not pledge your love to God? That would be a good pledge.

Now let's get back to the food laws.

> Turn to Leviticus 11:3–23, and you can read of the clean and unclean meats of animals that God tell us about! How much of the unclean have you been fed in your church?

³Whatsoever parteth the hoof, and is clovenfooted, and cheweth the cud, among the beasts, that shall ye eat. ⁴Nevertheless these shall ye not eat of them that chew the cud, or of them that divide the hoof: as the camel, because he cheweth the cud, but divideth not the hoof; he is unclean unto you. ⁵And the coney, because he cheweth the cud, but divideth not the hoof; he is unclean unto you. ⁶And the hare, because he cheweth the cud, but divideth not the hoof; he is unclean unto you. ⁷And the swine, though he divide the hoof, and be clovenfooted, yet he cheweth not the cud; he is unclean to you. ⁸Of their flesh shall ye not eat, and their carcase shall ye not touch; they are unclean to you. ⁹These shall ye eat of all that are in the waters: whatsoever hath fins and scales in the waters, in the seas, and in the rivers, them shall ye eat. ¹⁰And all that have not fins and scales in the seas, and in the rivers, of all that move in the waters, and of any living thing which is in the waters, they shall be an abomination unto you: ¹¹They shall be even an abomination unto you; ye shall not eat of their flesh, but ye shall have their carcases in abomination. ¹²Whatsoever hath no fins nor scales in the waters, that shall be an abomination unto you. ¹³And these are they which ye shall have in abomination among the fowls; they shall not be eaten, they are an abomination: the eagle, and the ossifrage, and the ospray, ¹⁴And the vulture, and the kite after his kind; ¹⁵Every raven after his kind; ¹⁶And the

owl, and the night hawk, and the cuckow, and the hawk after his kind, [17]And the little owl, and the cormorant, and the great owl, [18]And the swan, and the pelican, and the gier eagle, [19]And the stork, the heron after her kind, and the lapwing, and the bat. [20]All fowls that creep, going upon all four, shall be an abomination unto you. [21]Yet these may ye eat of every flying creeping thing that goeth upon all four, which have legs above their feet, to leap withal upon the earth; [22]Even these of them ye may eat; the locust after his kind, and the bald locust after his kind, and the beetle after his kind, and the grasshopper after his kind. [23]But all other flying creeping things, which have four feet, shall be an abomination unto you.

God's Food Laws

Clean	Unclean
Cattle	Camels
Deer	Rabbit
Fish with fins and scales	Horses and their kin
Quail	Squirrels, rats
Sheep and goats	Jack rabbit (cotton tail)
Chicken	Swine
Turkey	Catfish (bottom feeders without scales. They'll eat anything dead or alive, kind of like a swine.)
Some grasshoppers and crickets	All bottom feeders like shrimp, oysters, clams, lobster, crawfish, etc.
Other various four-legged jumpers	Eagle, seagull, owl, vulture, storks, bats and most birds.
	All web-footed birds, ducks, etc.
	Varmints, all beasts (monkeys, bears, dogs, cats, apes, etc.)

Always remember that you will *not* go to Hell for consuming these unclean meats, but because God made our bodies, He knows how they should be cared for by proper nourishment. Like I said before, if you won't follow the *simplest* of God's laws (the food laws), how can He depend upon you to obey and follow *any* of His laws? (Good luck to that!) God expects us to follow all of His laws as best we can. So do it! God demands it.

BELIEFS THAT ARE NOT TRUE

Let's discuss a few of the false beliefs that are widely accepted by some people who are uneducated in God's truth.

Belief 1: You Must be Born Again or I Am a Born-Again Christian

People show their ignorance when using this phrase. I'll explain. (Ignorance is not a bad word. It simply means that a person doesn't know.)

In John 3:3–7, we read:

> [3]Jesus answered and said unto him, Verily, verily [truly, truly] I say unto thee, Except a man be born again, he cannot see the kingdom of God. [4]Nicodemus saith unto him [Christ] How can a man be born when he is old? can he enter the second time into his mother's womb, and be born? [5]Jesus answered, Verily, verily [truly, truly] I say unto thee, Except a man be born of water and *of* the Spirit, he cannot enter into the kingdom of God.
> [6]That which is born of the flesh is flesh; and that which is born of the Spirit is spirit. [Jesus is still speaking here.] [7]Marvel not that I said unto thee, Ye must be born again.

Now let me show you how simple it is to clear the air by checking out the word *again* as quoted here in the New Testament. This word *again* is written in the Greek language.

In the Greek dictionary, *Strong's Exhaustive Concordance*, go to the Greek word *again* and you'll find it to be number 509; this is the Greek language number for the word. So what does the definition say? The answer says "born from above."

Now go back and read the third and seventh verses one more time and you'll be able to visualize the actual meaning of the word *again*.

Naturally, a person needs to be born "from above" to be able to return there.

You cannot be born "again" of the womb (nor anywhere else for that matter). Give it some serious thought, it'll come to you!

Belief 2: Once Saved, Always Saved

This is a false teaching that can cause a ton of damage concerning one's ultimate demise. It can cause a person to lose his very soul! It's a dangerous belief.

This statement needs a bunch of clarifications.

We'll start here: Our Father keeps a *book*, and *in* God's Book of Life is written every person's name. Beside our names, our *sins* are written one by one. Our good deeds and our works are written there too.

Our Father is the only person deserving, worthy, and pure enough to open this Book of Life. He is the judge as He says, "³And no man in heaven, nor in earth, neither under the earth, was able to open the book, neither to look thereon" (Revelations 5:3).

Further in Revelation 20:11–12, 14–15:

> ¹¹And I saw a great white throne, and him [our Father] that sat on it, from whose face the earth and the heaven fled away; and there was found no place for them. [The bright and majestic light that our Father emits] ¹²And I saw the dead [the dead means spiritually dead] small and great, stand before God; and the books were opened: and another book was opened, which is *the book* of life: and the dead [spiritually dead] were judged out of those things which were written in the books, according to their works.

¹⁴And death and hell were cast into the lake of fire. This is the second death. [This second death is the death of your soul and only God can destroy your soul. If you will repent, your soul will be saved. God is a "consuming fire" therefore He *becomes* that "lake of fire.] ¹⁵And whosoever was not found written in the book of life was cast into the lake of fire. [This will be the second death (the death of your soul). You exist no more. You are gone and even the *memory* of you is erased. That's why there will be no more tears.]

Our Father paid a hefty price on that cross. He died for *our* sins, not *His* sins (because He is sinless). This gift of repentance was given to us by Him, and it is the *blessing of all blessings.*

Our Father paid that price because He loves all of His children, and we must show our Father in Heaven that we love Him in return; we *must* daily utilize His gift of repentance by repenting sincerely to Him. By doing so, He will blot out those sins from the Book of Life and allow us a fresh and clean start.

But if a person neglects repentance, and when God opens that book with you standing right there in front of Him, and the book is filled with all the sins that you have committed but have *not* repented of, how do you think God is going to judge you?

This belief of "once save, always saved" will *not* save you. (But repentance will.)

You can see now that *you can backslide yourself right into Hell*, but if you repent that slate will be cleansed and blotted by God's forgiveness. (He never wants you to speak of that sin again because it has been blotted out. It exists no more.)

It's true enough that God does the saving, but, as always, in God's Word there are written stipulations for redemption.

As you read the Bible, you will run across the word *if.* That is a very *big* word because it's a condition. God tells us that He will do this or that *if* we'll do *our* part of His promise. So be sure that you always take the word *if* seriously.

You can make it to Heaven *if* you repent of all your sins. Now we can say, "Once saved, always saved *if* we repent."

Belief 3: Angels Have Wings

This is a false statement and it is so very easy to prove that it is total nonsense.

God says in Genesis 1:26, "²⁶And God said: Let us make man in our image, after our likeness: and let them have dominion over the fish of the sea, and over the fowl of the air, and over the cattle, and over all the earth, and over every creeping thing that creepeth upon the earth."

Who is God talking to in this verse? The answer: to his angels—us!

So on the sixth day God created man. Do we have wings? Answer: No! Since we are created in the exact likeness of them they then have *no* wings either. (*Wings* are simply man's silly imagination.) End of story!

Belief 4: God Has blessings, Not Curses

God has blessed us, the people, with this majestic and abundant land here in North America. We should thank Him daily for this wonderful gift.

I like the way Moses prayed concerning our land (which actually belongs to our Father).

Moses said (in his prayer to God): "¹⁵Look down from thy holy habitation, from heaven, and bless thy people Israel [(that's us],) and the land which thou hast given us, as thou swarest [(promised]) unto our fathers, a land that floweth with milk and honey" (Deuteronomy 26:15).

Why did God give us this great land? Answer: Because He loves us.

He says: "¹⁹And to make thee high above all nations which he hath made, in praise, and in name, and in honour; and that thou mayest be an holy people unto the LORD thy God, as he hath spoken. [The United States of America did not just happen. God planned this long ago]" (Deuteronomy 26:19).

In this verse, we can see that God has kept *His* part of the deal, but how about our part?

Are we Holy People?

Do we magnify our Father's name?

Do we follow His laws (even His food laws)?

Do we even believe that there *is* a God?

Do we *deserve any* blessings from God?

Do we hold our morals in high esteem?

Do we want to take the *name of God* out of everything?

Do we cater instead to *misfits* to appease them in the name of political correctness?

All of God's blessings come with conditions. God says He will do this *if* we will do that, which is more than fair. God is always fair, and we, the people, need to recognize his fairness and be as fair to Him in return. But by our truthful consideration and truthful answers to these eight questions above, you can easily see that we have miserably failed our Father.

God has given us the e*quation* to peace, happiness, joy, and success *if* we would do things *His* way!

What is the equation?

What is the word *if?*

(In the following verses from Deuteronomy 28:1–14, God is telling us the blessings that will come about *if* we do our part of the equation.)

This is the equation! As you read, catch the *ifs*. These statements are unconditional.

> [1]And it shall come to pass, if thou shalt hearken diligently [seriously] unto the voice of the LORD thy God, to observe and to do all his commandments which I command thee this day, that the LORD thy God will set thee on high above all nations of the earth: [2]And all these blessings shall come on thee, and overtake [overwhelm] thee, if

thou shalt hearken unto the voice of the Lord thy God. ³Blessed shalt thou be in the city, and blessed shalt thou be in the field. ⁴Blessed shall be the fruit of thy body [our children] and the fruit of thy ground, and the fruit of thy cattle, the increase of thy kine, and the flocks of thy sheep. ⁵Blessed shall be thy basket [our storehouses to store our abundance of food, grains, etc.] and thy store. [Store means our kneading-troughs for our dough. Maybe like our bakeries of today.] ⁶Blessed shalt thou be when thou comest in, and blessed shalt thou be when thou goest out. [God is saying: I'll bless you coming and going.] ⁷The Lord shall cause thine enemies that rise up against thee to be smitten before thy face: they shall come out against thee one way, and flee before thee seven ways. [Because of our superior armed forces.] ⁸The Lord shall command [order] the blessing upon thee in thy torehouses, and in all that thou settest thine hand unto; and he shall bless thee in the land which the Lord thy God giveth thee. ⁹The Lord shall establish thee an holy people unto himself, as he hath sworn unto thee, if thou shalt keep the commandments of the Lord thy God, and walk in his ways. ¹⁰And all people of the earth shall see that thou art called by the name of the Lord; and they shall be afraid of thee. [God wanted us to set the example.] ¹¹And the Lord shall make thee plenteous in goods, in the fruit of thy body [our children] and in the fruit of thy cattle, and in the fruit of thy ground, in the land which the Lord sware unto thy fathers to give thee. ¹²The Lord shall open unto thee his good treasure, the heaven to give the rain unto thy land in his season, and to bless all the work of thine hand: and thou shalt lend unto many nations, and thou shalt not borrow. [It'll rain when He wants it to rain.] ¹³And the Lord shall make thee the head, and not the tail; and thou shalt be above only, and thou shalt not be beneath; if that thou hearken unto the commandments of the Lord thy God, which I command thee this day, to observe and to do them: ¹⁴And thou shalt not go aside from any of the words which I command thee this day, to the right hand, or to the left, to go after other gods to serve them.

Now that we've covered a few of God's promises to us through His blessings and doing His part, what has He promised to do now since we failed on our end?

The answer is quite simple: He now, as we speak, is in the midst of giving us a showering of curses (and we deserve them all!).

Now God is going to tell us about the curses that we'll endure *if* we do not follow His commandments. As He says in Deuteronomy 27:15–26:

> [15]Cursed be the man that maketh any graven or molten image, an abomination unto the LORD, the work of the hands of the craftsman, and putteth it in a secret place. And all the people shall answer and say, Amen. [16]Cursed be he that setteth light by his father or his mother. And all the people shall say, Amen. [17]Cursed be he that removeth his neighbour's landmark. And all the people shall say, Amen. [18]Cursed be he that maketh the blind to wander out of the way. And all the people shall say, Amen. [19]Cursed be he that perverteth the judgment of the stranger, fatherless, and widow. And all the people shall say, Amen. [20]Cursed be he that lieth with his father's wife; because he uncovereth his father's skirt. And all the people shall say, Amen. [21]Cursed be he that lieth with any manner of beast. And all the people shall say, Amen. [22]Cursed be he that lieth with his sister, the daughter of his father, or the daughter of his mother. And all the people shall say, Amen. [23]Cursed be he that lieth with his mother in law. And all the people shall say, Amen. [24]Cursed be he that smiteth his neighbour secretly. And all the people shall say, Amen. [25]Cursed be he that taketh reward to slay an innocent person. And all the people shall say, Amen. [26]Cursed be he that confirmeth not all the words of this law to do them. And all the people shall say, Amen.

Further in Deuteronomy 28:15–22:

> [13]But it shall come to pass, if thou wilt not hearken unto the voice of the LORD thy God, to observe to do all his commandments and his statutes [laws] which I command thee this day; [and He means this day] that all these curses shall come upon thee, and overtake [overwhelm] thee: [16]Cursed shalt thou be in the city, and cursed shalt thou be in the field.
>
> [17]Cursed shall be thy basket and thy store. [18]Cursed shall be the fruit of thy body, and the fruit of thy land, the increase of thy kine, and the flocks of thy sheep. [19]Cursed shalt thou be when thou comest in, and cursed shalt thou be when thou goest out. [20]The LORD shall send upon thee cursing, vexation, and rebuke, in all that thou settest thine hand unto for to do, until thou be destroyed, and until thou perish quickly; because of the wickedness of thy doings, whereby thou hast forsaken me. [21]The LORD shall make the pestilence cleave unto thee, until he have consumed thee from off the land, whither thou goest to possess it.
>
> [22]The LORD shall smite thee with a consumption, and with a fever, and with an inflammation, and with an extreme burning, and with the sword, and with blasting, and with mildew; and they shall pursue thee until thou perish.

God can be, oh, so very vengeful when we disobey Him. Do you think we are disobeying Him in our land, in our country? Look around and observe! You bet we're disobeying Him big time!

We are taking God out of everything we can to appease a minority of crackpots like atheists, homosexuals, and agnostics, and by listening to and electing and putting lawmakers in power who are nothing but socialistic and communistic acting nuts— acting like idiotic children.

Do you know that God told us this would happen? He stated this 3,500 years ago. It was a prophecy then, and it is coming true exactly as it is written. God's prophecies *always* come to pass!

On your own, get your Bible—the King James Version—and read the remainder verses of Deuteronomy 28, and you'll easily see that God has replaced the blessings with *curses*, and who can blame Him? We've done it ourselves.

Just think: Our world would have been one huge *garden of perfection* had we simply followed Him. Do you remember that I quoted Christ a few pages back, when He said, "Follow me"? He not only said it, but He meant it. Are we truly following Him? Answer: *No.*

God's laws are being broken in our churches, our schools, our government, and in our very homes—everywhere.

But people are going to *know* in this generation that there *is* a God. It is apparent, through the actions and deeds of the people, that they really and truly do not believe He even exists. I truly believe this. (May God bless those of us that *keep* Him in the equation of our lives.)

What a sad state of affairs we are in by *not* following God. It weighs heavy on my heart, and I'm but one mere mortal. Just think how God—our closest of kin and our very creator—must be feeling right now. If you have any compassion at all in your heart, soul, and mind, you'd automatically know and understand that he is hurting big-time. His disappointment in us is *big-time*. (We'll all see His vengeance soon. *Correction* is just around the corner, and *all* of the wrongs *will* be made right.)

My wish is that all peoples would *wake up* and be filled with shame and do their dead level best to turn things around and become that true Christian nation that God expects us to be. I guess we're too stubborn to do that; it appears pride and haughtiness now rules this country. Everything is money, money, money and more money!

The politicians lie awake at night trying to dream up some new tax to hang us out to dry some new lie to cram down our throats, some new burden of corruption to lay on us along with new lies after new lies after new lies, blah, blah, blah, blah—you get the point. Corruption runs wild from the White House to the House and to the Senate and almost all of the branches of government. Morals are out the window. It seems that our lawmakers vote *yea* to enact bills into law that they haven't even read! Surely!

Does anyone remember anything about Rome? How about Sodom and Gomorrah? How about the Flood? Remember these? (God's wrath is furious.) God *is* watching! Beware! God is preparing at this time to eradicate *all* evil off the face of the earth. He's tired of it!

If people truly *do* remember, why do they keep on and on with the same old sins by mocking God this way. God *will not* be mocked! God *will not* be snubbed! God created Hell-fire for a reason! God *is* that "consuming fire," and God *is* grieving! Can you blame Him?

God's mercy is running thin. So Beware!

None of the above is open for debate because *fact is fact!*

Facts leave *no* room for debates.

God's Word is always the final word; God has a cup and it is called *the cup of wrath*. God is bringing this *cup of wrath* with Him upon His Second Coming, and I can promise you that He is coming to pour that *cup of wrath* out on all the evilness and evildoers on the face of this earth, and the time is near. The warning whistles are being blown, can you hear them?

I hope these evil politicians who burden the innocent get theirs first! God detests people who put burdens upon His children. It is a direct abuse of power. How can these people call themselves Christians and act in this manner? (In this case, a person *can* really "judge a book by its cover.")

They absolutely show no compassion for the people, and so God will show no compassion for them as *true justice* is poured out upon them. They have brought this sentence upon themselves, and the people that voted them in are just as guilty. (Many people yearn for a *true Christian* as a representative in our government. Is it too little too late?) It may be too late to change the direction of our country, but it is *never* too late for true repentance.

God's wrath is at a boiling point. His anger is riled.

God says—as He always does best—in Isaiah 13:6–9, 11:

> 6Howl ye; [listen up] for the day of the LORD is at hand; it *shall* come as a destruction from the Almighty. [Yes, it is payback time!] 7Therefore shall all hands be faint, and every man's heart shall melt: [The evil mortals. Are *you* an evil mortal?] Mortal means, "liable to die." 8And they shall be afraid: pangs and sorrows shall take hold of them; they shall be in pain as a woman that travaileth: [like labor pains] they shall be amazed one at another; their faces shall be as flames. 9Behold, the day of the LORD cometh, cruel [stern justice] both with wrath and fierce anger, [can you blame Him?] to lay the land desolate: and he shall destroy the sinners thereof out of it. [The habitual sinners, are you one?] 11And I *will* punish the world for their evil, and the wicked for their iniquity; and I will cause the arrogancy of the proud to cease, and will lay low the haughtiness of the terrible.

Notice that I have emphasized *shall* and *will*; God did not say, "*maybe* I'm going to do this." He says, "I *shall* do these things."

Now the question remains; do you believe God's Word?

Take a personal inventory of your beliefs. If a person *truly* believes God's Word, why do they not practice it? (The truth is in the pudding!) If you quack like a duck, then you've got to be a duck! I feel sorry for you sitting ducks out there because payday is right around the corner. Enjoy!

Amen.

LEARN GOD'S WORD
(DON'T BE A FOOL)

In the beginning, God created all of the planets. All the stars we see were placed there in the universe by Him and Him alone. He needed no help. If you think of the majestic beauty of the heavenly space that is above us, it becomes an impossibility to fathom the power of our Heavenly Father, the creator of everything, even the air we breathe.

The Bible doesn't tell us how long ago "the beginning" is, but science teaches us that it was eons ago, and it is true.

In comparison, all of mankind should be astonished at the massive power of our almighty Father who created us all. Every one of us is His creation—every race, color, or creed. He *owns* our souls that are inside these flesh bodies, and He can do anything He chooses with us. He also gave us free will. We can choose to *love Him* or we can choose to *hate Him* by ignoring His true teachings to us, but that would be a *big mistake* on our part.

It seems that it would be a no-brainer for every one of us to love and adore Him, our Creator, but the bad news is that most people *don't* worship Him. It's easy to *say* that you love Him, but in actuality it's just words. You may just *think* you love him, but do you tell Him that you love Him? When is the last time you talked to Him?

I've read surveys where 80–88 percent of the people in our country claim to be Christians. Oh, really? I do believe that the majority *think* and *believe* there is a God—but it just ends there.

How many people do you know that you can sit down with and discuss God's Word as it is written? Do you know why you can rarely find one person? It's because they haven't studied God's letter to us, the Bible. They have no clue what is inside. They haven't been taught God's actual truth. Their Bibles just sit there in the house gathering dust. (I like to think about the Bible as a "how to" book of instructions. It's like the instructions inside some things we buy today; without reading those instructions, we may not be able to understand how it's supposed to be put together and work.) The Bible though teaches us how to put together and maintain a worry-free life while here in these flesh bodies, as well as how to have an everlasting life—a life with *no* end.

The same is true with God's instructions to us on how to do almost any thing. He tells us things that we should *not eat* (Leviticus 11). He tells about the things that we should and shouldn't do and about His blessing and curses. He tells us how to be happy in these flesh bodies (entirety of Ecclesiastes) and warns us of the many pitfalls to avoid during our journey through this second earth age. He teaches and instructs us how to travail His universe and come out a winner, that is, a big-time winner. He also tells us how to come out a loser (a big-time loser respectively as well). He tells who to listen and who not listen to. He promises us that He'll send us teachers so that we can be properly taught in order to gain vital understanding of His word. He teaches us how to be happy and how to *never* worry; God is so good to us. He loves us.

He gives us a very valuable gift and it's called *discernment*. He expects us to use this gift all through our lives. The use of *discernment* and the gifts of *free will* and *common sense* will take us down the right path when used seriously.

These gifts can also become a serious liability when used incorrectly.

God has "foretold us all things," haven't you read? It is written.

The purpose of this writing is to nudge you into wanting to learn the wisdom of His holy Word. Since all wisdom comes from God, doesn't it make sense that we should learn and love His instructions so that we can receive His blessings and promises?

Did you know that our Father *cannot lie?* Think about that. He *cannot lie* or lead us down the wrong path because it's absolutely and virtually impossible for Him to do that for He *is* Truth! (I found that many years ago when I needed a teacher—a true teacher blessed with the talent of teaching with true understanding.) Your personal pastor should be your preacher, but most of them do not have enough knowledge of God's Word to teach you much of anything.

I believe that most people can read the Bible in its entirety over and over and still won't come to much knowledge of God's Word on his own. The Bible has to be taught chapter by chapter, line by line, precept by precept, and book by book as God instructs.

If you can find a teacher who can really give you the correct interpretations of the Bible, then he is gifted indeed, and *you* are very fortunate and blessed beyond words.

When God's Word is interpreted *correctly* (and you follow these interpretations daily so that these don't slip away), they will stay with you throughout your life. Your *life* will be blessed. I know that life is not a cakewalk, but to be able to go through this second earth age, with God's wisdom is a beautiful thing.

The big problems won't be so big anymore; doom will cease to exist in your mind as you'll finally realize that you are a child of God—a living and loving God. (I chose to seek truth and to be a partaker of His many blessings. Won't you as well?)

If you choose to be a fool, you should read Proverbs 12:15, "[15]The way of a fool *is* right in his own eyes: but he that hearkeneth unto counsel *is* wise".

Do you want to be a fool or do you want to be wise? You do have free will to decide which pathway to take. I'd strongly advise you to seek God's wisdom because the path of a fool is *dismal*!

Put your trust in God! Don't be a fool.

Amen.

5

TEN WAYS TO TRUE SALVATION
(A SERIOUS MESSAGE TO MY READERS)

The road to salvation—*true* salvation—is really quite simple. There is nothing complex about God's Word. He makes it easy for us to understand.

Follow these rules:

1. You must *want* to be saved. Saved from what? *Answer*: Saved from being *blotted out* thus not being qualified to be a partaker of the beautiful and peaceful never-ending Heaven that our Creator has prepared for us who wish to be there to enjoy. There will be peace and joy far beyond our deepest imaginations! Who in their right mind would want to miss it? Only a fool.

2. To show yourself approved, you must delve *feet first* into His word. What word? *Answer*: God's Word, *not* man's word. Men can mislead you; God will not mislead you. So, you may ask, how can I find a teacher to teach me the actual truth, not lies? I've told you in this book that the only place that I have found to *learn God's full truth*

is to watch and listen to Shepherd's Chapel. (Just look at your TV listings and you'll find it.) Be sincere and don't miss *any* of the lectures, take notes, get the necessary reference books to back up these truths from the original manuscripts. It is simple and foolproof. Don't wait, get started now. (You'll never know tomorrow can be one day too late.)

3. You need to take these studies seriously because God takes *you* seriously. *He knows* if you are being sincere. You cannot fool Him in any manner! You must *believe*. (*Without* true faith you are wasting your time!)

4. As you learn the truths of God's Word and become a *true* believer, simply ask God for forgiveness of all your previous sins—and truly mean it—and ask His mercy by accepting you into His loving arms of protection. Don't become some kind of religious nut. Always protect your credibility. That *is* doing thing's God's way!

5. Now that you have been accepted by our Heavenly Father, you must continuously study and do it as a daily routine. Don't worry, you'll become eager to never miss a day without adding something to your knowledge. You'll see. (Remember, watch Shepherd's Chapel daily. Never miss a lecture.)

6. Always be careful whom you listen to. Don't listen to lies and don't attend a church or support a church that constantly begs for money. They do not actually care about you or your soul; they are after your money. Trust me, this is truly all they *really* want. They are not of God, and God didn't send them. They are deceivers. They are workers of Satan. Stay away from them.

7. Be consistent as you study God's letter—the King James Version only—to *us*, and you will find that you are *not alone*. God's Holy Spirit will be with you, and you will actually *feel* that spiritual closeness, and *always* be sure to thank Him for allowing His Spirit to come into your

mind. *He knows* when you are truly *trying* and that counts as 100 percent to Him. So, get busy. Time is short.

Remember: You must be *consistent* in studying God's Word. If you are not totally consistent, then God will doubt your sincerity. So don't do that! Don't run hot and then cold.

8. People must *change* the direction of their lives in most cases and that is a good thing! Take inventory of your acquaintances, and if they are influencing you in a negative way then stay away from them as far as you can—which you must. Simply and quietly set them aside. Don't treat them as enemies; don't ever do that. Just set an example, and you'll be surprised at the positive influence that you'll "emit" toward them. They may not admit it, but in the back of their minds they will want some of the *good stuff* (the blessings) that the people who try enjoy daily. (God's Words are fantastic!) Never preach to them; simply set an example. Remember always to protect your credibility at all times. (The world has way too many religious nuts running around out there—so never be a *part* of them and avoid them.)

9. *Repent* daily. Don't miss a day for that! Keep your name that is written in God's book of judgment—the Book of Life—clean. Jesus Christ died for our sins so that you could have *repentance*, so, by all means, use it. *Repentance* is the gift of *all* gifts. When you repent, and sincerely mean it, God erases those sins from the book at that very moment; and He told us to never bring those sins up again. So *never* bring them up again! I have noticed in life that many people have the problem of not forgiving themselves. You must forgive yourself to have that *fresh start*.

10. *Be considerate* of others and *their* individual beliefs. (I can tell you now in the world today that most religions and denominations out there in no way coincide with God's Word.) These people are simply "playing church." Let them

live in their arrogance of ignorance. They have so much nonsense drilled into their gray matter that they'd never listen to you anyway. (If they love that highway to Hell, let them travel on!) Consideration produces kindness. A true Christian is considerate and kind. They have *heart*. A true Christian is always *upbeat* and of a positive attitude. Why? Because we know that we are doing things God's way as best as we can.

Never forget that your *works* while here in the flesh is the one and only thing that you can take with you when you die. The only thing! So try, if possible, to be of help to anyone who asks. Always be discerning in all things. Don't be someone's *fool*. You can walk proudly. Why? Because you are a *child of God* who knows truth!

Have compassion for others; it is an excellent work. *Compassion and consideration* run hand-in-hand and many offshoots of good work come from those two words. Keep those two words in your heart and in your mind. In your practices and your deeds always strive to do the *right things* in your everyday lives. Don't be a hypocrite, a "play actor." Never become a self-righteous hypocrite; the world is full of them too. God hates hypocrites.

This is truly the last generation. All prophecies *will* come to pass in this generation. The sixth trump is right around the corner, and Satan will appear *claiming to be* "Jesus Christ our Savior," and the whole world—except us—will whore after him. Don't go there!

Five months later after this, the seventh trump will usher in, bringing the *real* Jesus Christ, our *true* Savior.

How you react to the sixth and the seventh trumps holds the true key to salvation. If you fall off the true path in the sixth trump instead of waiting for the *true Christ* at the seventh trump, you'll have yourself a real bad problem. A great big problem! So don't fall of the true path.

Deception is truly Satan's lethal weapon! Don't let him use that weapon on you! Come out of confusion. There is no need to be deceived. Simply do all things in God's way as best as you can. If you mess up, repent to God, and move on! He is very, very, very understanding. He loves you.

The last three trumps (learn these).

Trumps represent a span of time. We are in the fifth trump now, which is God's time for teaching and learning.

At the end of the fifth span of time—which is quickly approaching—the sixth span of time begins; and it presents the coming of the fake Jesus who is Satan himself in live and living color. It is only for a duration of *five months*. You can easily, as a true Christian, handle it with no problem.

Then at the seventh and final trump, the real Jesus Christ will appear, and we are *all* changed instantly back into our spiritual bodies. *Wait for the real Jesus*! Don't let Satan sway you over to his camp. He is a lying fake—a phony. Don't even listen to him when he comes. (Isn't that now easy to understand? I surely hope so. You've got a leg up on almost all people just by knowing this!)

Share this information if the opportunity arises. The fact that Satan is coming, claiming to *be* Christ is going to catch most, if not *all*, people off guard.

Always remember this truth: By using (1) discernment, you will show that you have (2) common sense. (3) Self-control brings about (4) sincerity and (5) honesty, which in turn brings forth (6) credibility showing that you possess (7) sound doctrine. Thus finally proving that you are a (8) true Christian.

(In Biblical numeric, *seven* means spiritual completeness, and *eight* means new beginnings.)

SATAN AND HIS LIES

Satan was created by God a long time ago on the first earth age. He was created just as we were. God made him the "full pattern." He's a *looker*. Satan is alive today just as we are. Actually no one has died yet. (For now, only the flesh dies off.)

As time passed, God elevated him to a high position: protector of the mercy seat. But one day Satan decided he wanted to be God and sit on that throne himself. And so began the *controversy* of today.

He calls himself God too. He feels confident that he'll win this controversy of *good versus evil*. He really and truly believes in his heart and mind that he can defeat God, our very Creator.

Guess what—he's doing an excellent and convincing job. God is allowing Satan to persuade all the people he can to follow him. God wants to know who in the end we'll choose. He or Satan?

Let's begin with *politics*:

Our political system is running over with liars, egomaniacs, greed, pride, evilness, taxation (even taxes on taxes), and ignorant laws designed to take away *our* freedoms and God's influence.

The politicians are running amuck with stupidity. We have politicians with a let-them-eat-cake attitude.

In my lifetime, I've never seen as much foolishness, bad laws, cronyism, and just plain nonsense.

God told us—yes He told *us*—the inhabitants of this "promised land" to *not* borrow money from other countries; and now look at the mess we're in.

Our so-called leaders *call* themselves "Christians." Oh really! Can you call yourself a Christian who add burdens on top of burdens on the citizens?

Same as Satan, almost all are phonies. They are doing his work for him. Satan has them eating out of his hand.

If I could judge these nuts, I'd throw them all out (all but a few). Most of these liberal-minded idiots need to find a new profession and stay out of the *burden* business!

There is no place for socialism in the United States.

These nuts stay in power because of the people who want their monthly handouts.

Some are too lazy to work but not too lazy to hold those hands out and say, "Gimmie, gimmie, gimmie." (The *truly* handicapped people are excluded.)

I've noticed that some of these lazy people are seriously obese nasty slobs because of *over*indulgence, not *under*indulgence! They are fatter because they eat more.

My adopted mother (who was born in 1887) once told me, "A good depression never hurt anyone. Don't worry about these people, they'll find a way to feed themselves. God built these bodies to seek nourishment."

Oh, how true! Entitlement is the word of the day. What a shame! Satan's influence is in the middle of it all, and he is doing an excellent job! People will follow him for a freebie (just like a puppy will obey you if you entice him with a little treat).

If you want to run for office and campaign on freebies, you'll most likely win the election. Join Satan and go for it; it appears that most of the politicians are on his bandwagon!

I believe an *intent* to ruin our nation is underway. I liken it to treason. And here again the negative influence of Satan is at work. His job is to tear down, not build up.

As the people in power weaken our armed forces, they are putting us in an awkward position on the world stage. I realize the technology that we have created in turn may create a lack of need for many more boots on the ground. Our proposed plan of war strategy should not be announced to the world. Many things are better left unsaid.

This country is being run by the minds of children. Isaiah 3:3–5 will tell you that God told us that this would come to pass in these end times. If people would have educated themselves in the things that God has warned us of, these things would *not* have taken place.

Many things are written in God's Word as an example to us so that we can avoid these many pitfalls, but people do not heed these warnings because as Christ often said, "Haven't you read? It is written."

God tells us that He has foretold us all things. Nothing is God's fault. The fault lies with us, the people. People don't heed God's Word because they don't know what it is. People are satisfied to believe any and everything their church leader tells them, and in many, many cases, these "simple listeners" will lose their souls in Hell. Why? Because of ignorance of God's Word. People do not study!

God has even said that "my people are a little bit sottish," which means a *little bit stupid*. My plea to you is to wake up and educate yourselves to reality! Time is quickly fading away. You've got to know that. You *must* believe that.

Christianity is a reality, not a religion.

You either believe God's word in its entirety or you don't believe it at all—and that's a *fact*.

You cannot take a little here and a little there and achieve the full scope of God's truth.

God's Word is a *recipe to salvation*. If you don't mix in the truth—the whole truth—in your mind, you will end up with a mishmash or nothingness; and that's another *fact*. Ask yourself, "When is the last time I opened my Bible?"

God has told us that He will send us teachers and prophets, and He has done just that. The Bible contains the *true* words and prophecies directly from God to these teachers and prophets.

Many so-called preachers have come in "God's name"; but are you sharp enough to distinguish whether they are telling you the real truth, or are they filling your head with lies? (God, most likely, didn't send them at all.)

Do you know the difference? You had better! Your *hereafter* depends upon your personal knowledge that God teaches. No preacher or church can save you. Only *you* can do that. (Work it out with God. It's personal between you and our Father.)

God has given us *the gift of discernment*, and He expects us to use it. The stuff that comes out of the mouths of nearly all—99.9 percent—of these so-called preachers that you see and hear are lies. Sounds harsh? Too bad! But it's a *fact*. The *harsh truth* should be an eye-opener to everyone. Most preachers whom people listen to don't care about the demise of your soul, but what they *really* care about is the demise of your wallets. Money, money, money—gimmie, gimmie, gimmie!

God says that they are an abomination, so don't listen to nor support them. God tells us that if we support them, "we become a part of their evil deeds."

God tells us to be very careful who and what we listen to. Trash in, trash out; lies in, lies out—from generation to generation they continue. That's why I tell you that Satan is excellent at deception. He's the king of deception! Deception, truly, is Satan's most lethal weapon!

False preachers (and I'll bet that *they* know this in their own hearts) are no better than a cold-blooded murderer. Their messages can easily cause a person's soul to perish if you *believe* their lies *and support* their lies by aiding them with your money. Don't do that.

Don't live in ignorance and confusion. *Truth* will set you free. God loves you and wants you. Salvation is free for the taking!

Quit being deceived! Life in the flesh is but a flash in the pan; so get with the program!

Give the following *common false teachings* your consideration and learn the truth, not fiction. Learn what God says, not man's imaginations or traditions. Traditions of men will lead you to la-la land.

1. Do you believe your pastor's sermons when they teach the rapture? Why would you? God teaches that it's an abomination to teach that nonsense or even to believe it. Read on what God says in Ezekiel 13:20–23:

> 20Wherefore thus saith the Lord GOD; Behold, I am against your pillows, wherewith ye there hunt the souls to make them fly, and I will tear them from your arms, and will let the souls go, even the souls that ye hunt to make them fly. 21Your kerchiefs also will I tear, and deliver my people out of your hand, and they shall be no more in your

hand to be hunted; and ye shall know that I am the Lord. [22]Because with lies ye have made the heart of the righteous sad, whom I have not made sad; and strengthened the hands of the wicked, that he should not return from his wicked way, by promising him life: [23]Therefore ye shall see no more vanity, nor divine *divinations*: for I will deliver my people out of your hand: and ye shall know that I am the Lord.

God tells us that He hates the teaching of fly-to-save-your-soul nonsense. Where do you think you're going to fly off to? Some cloud in the "sky"? God tell us to *stand*, not fly, fly away. Heaven is going to be right here on earth, not somewhere off in la-la land! God gave us common sense, so use it.

Now read Ephesians 6:11, "[11]Put on the whole armour of God, that ye may be able to *stand* [not fly] against the wiles of the devil [and never ever forget it]."

At the sixth trump, Satan will come to earth and tell you that *he is God himself* and his message will be that *I've come to* fly *you out of here. Let's go! Hurry now!*

Many have been taught that they should want to be the first ones to be taken, but God instructs you to *stand*! Go back and read Ephesians 6:11.

The "armor" is God's Word. Put it on real good. Wear it with pride. If you support a church that teaches you the rapture lie, run away as fast as you can. They're lying to you! It's nonsense!

The rapture teaching cannot be found in God's Word anywhere because it's false.

Satan wants to *be* God, and people aren't being taught that Satan comes in the sixth trump. Christ comes at the seventh trump, only five months later. We are all changed back into our angelic bodies in the blink of an eye. When Satan returns we are still in our flesh bodies. See how easy it is to tell who's who?

If you stick with believing that rapture fairy tale, you'll receive the keys to the wrong gates: the gates to Hell.

Get away from and never support—tithe to—a so-called church that teaches garbage like that. Learn scholarship. Learn truth. If you support a church that teaches that rapture stuff, you become a partaker of their evil deeds. God prophesied this way back around AD 90.

In 2 John 1:10–11, it is written that "¹⁰If there come any unto you, and bring not this doctrine, receive him not into your house, neither bid him God speed: ¹¹For he that biddeth him God speed is partaker of his evil deeds."

A mentally ill woman preacher dreamed the rapture theory up around the mid- 1800s. Her name was Margaret McDonald, and the preachers just ate it up and began spreading the rapture to their church members (to draw a bigger crowd, I suppose, so they could *pass the plate* more often to bring in more bucks!).

I call it a tickle-your-ears teaching. It sounds like an easy way with an early out but it is simply a false teaching, a lie. (Wow, these false church leaders are really going to "love" me for exposing them and their lies, aren't they?)

2. Maybe you were taught that Eve tempted Adam with an apple from the tree of good and evil. As you'll recall, God told them *not* to partake of that tree, but being of the flesh, their human bodies are subject to their lusts—so they just had to try it. (How sad that our children are taught this phone-apple story in Sunday Schools all across America.)

But do you know what or who they actually partook of?

It was Satan himself. They were totally seduced by Satan. (You've got an imagination enough to understand what went on there.) Christ Himself in His own words tells us in John 8:44–47,

> ⁴⁴Ye [Christ speaking of Cain's offspring] are of your father the devil, and the lusts of your father ye will do. He was a murderer from the beginning, and abode not in the truth, because there is no truth in him. When he speaketh a lie, he speaketh of his own: for he is a liar, and the father of it.

[45]Because I tell you the truth, ye believe me not. Which of you convinceth me of sin? And if I say the truth, why do ye not believe me? [47]He that is of God heareth God's words: ye therefore hear them not, because ye are not of God.

And this saying of Christ brings us to:

3. Cain and Abel who were born twins. However the father of Cain is Satan while the father of Abel is Adam. "[2]And she again bare his brother Abel. And Abel was a keeper of sheep, but Cain was a tiller of the ground" (Genesis 4:2). "Again" is the third word of the verse. The Hebrew manuscript's translation is "continued." When a woman continues in labor after one birth, it means that she is having yet another child.

Two fathers is no mystery at all. (Your family doctor will tell you that although rare, this can be true in pregnancies.)

There is much more to be written about Cain: His offspring is the Kenites—Satan's kin—thus God's enemies.

4. Easter is one of the most celebrated events of the year. Moms and Dads boil and dye eggs and buy all the cute little clothing for the babies. Then all the children can hide, hunt, and gather all these eggs and put them in their pretty little Easter baskets.

It really is quite a ritual that is celebrated and worshiped throughout the so-called Christian world; but this celebration is *not* of God. I repeat, *not* of God. It is an abomination! It's evil.

Churches of all religions go all-out for the great day of the Lord, but they are celebrating these traditions of men out of pure ignorance—*ignorance of God's words of truth.*

People do not realize the sin that they are committing. They don't realize what they are doing is hated by our Father on high. This tradition has been passed on from generation to generation, and a lack of education of God's Word is at the root of it all—and that is just plain sad!

This is the deceptive work of Satan himself. Yes, Satan has wormed his way into the pulpits of the world!

What a shame that pastors are sucked in to this erroneous celebration practice that they call Easter and yet they call themselves pastors. Pastors are supposed to feed the truth to their flock, not fairy tales! Easter is a fairy tale but Passover is *truth*— it is a *fact*.

Easter celebration began long ago as a sexual ritual every spring; sexual orgies out in the woods and doing every sexually evil acts one can imagine. The evil sexual goddess, Ishtar, was the queen of it all, and this celebration has worked its way into our houses of worship. Don't these pastors realize that Easter is a pagan holiday? Don't they realize that it is a satanic practice? Because the pastors are ignorant of God's Word, they are practicing the traditions of men. God has warned us over and over to stay away from traditions. (Hey pastors, celebrate Passover! There is *no* other way but God's way.)

Now, look up the word Easter (Ishtar) in any good *Webster's College Edition Dictionary* and see for yourselves the meaning of it. Ishtar was a *sexual goddess* leading this satanic celebration of spring.

It is an abomination to God for this teaching to be brought into a church that calls itself a "house of God," but yet it continues.

I marvel at man's stupidity and false traditions!

Passover should be *the celebration* of celebrations because Christ *became* our Passover, which is the highest *holy day* of the year! He died on the cross for us, and Christ did not mention anything about Easter eggs as He was nailed to the cross. Christ shed that blood for us as He quoted Psalms 22. The word *Easter* is used only once in the Acts of the Apostles 12:4, "And when he had apprehended him, he put him in prison, and delivered him to four quaternions of soldiers to keep him; intending after Easter to bring him forth to the people." Take the word *Easter* back to the Greek manuscripts and you'll find *Pascha*; therefore, it should properly be called Passover, not Easter. A false translator slipped in the word *Easter*. The scribe, no doubt, was a Kenite. We'll discuss *Kenites* later.

Our Father intends us to worship Him and Him only— not a springtime sexual goddess named Ishtar and her *fast* little Easter bunny beliefs along with the sexual orgies that she practiced. It's a direct slap to God's face to celebrate this nonsense. Wake up!

Do things God's way, not Satan's. God's meaning of Passover is—and always will be—to place (symbolically) the blood of the Lamb (Christ) over our door posts so that all things satanic and evil will see that we are *true* Christians and will *pass* over us and our homes, thus *Passover*. Get it? You notice that Easter celebrations and boiling eggs and Easter parades are never mentioned in our Father's word! It is pure and simple blasphemy.

You'll notice that there is no mention of sexual orgies (Easter) or Ishtar, little fast bunnies, eggs, Easter baskets, Easter bonnets, and all such nonsense. This practice is a disgrace to our Father. It's a downright slap in the face of our Heavenly Father, and that is not a wise thing to do.

Passover is all about Christ's blood that He shed for you and me, and His coming back again, to prove to us that He defeated death, which is to say, Satan.

This is a very serious injustice to our Heavenly Father. *Quit* doing that satanic stuff and learn the truth! Get those Satan-inspired rituals out of your churches. Don't be an abomination to our Living God but instead be a church that He'll approve of. Be pleasing to God. Don't follow man's divine divinations that are stupid dreams. Do God's way and have His blessings.

Passover always falls on the fifteenth day past the spring equinox when spring season begins. It doesn't matter what day of the week it falls on because *that day* is Passover, *the highest day* of worship to our Heavenly Father or in other words *the high day of Christianity*. So, celebrate *Passover*. Quit celebrating Satan's evil day, Easter—it's nonsense!

These truths are not up for debate. Truth is truth and lies are lies!

Be pleasing to God and follow His most *high day* for *true* Christians. Don't be deceived!

Deception, truly, is Satan's lethal weapon.

5. The controversy between God and Satan.

God created Satan the *full pattern*. God made him a real good looking supernatural being, and Satan did an excellent job for our Father. Satan did *so* good that he was elevated to the position of protector of the mercy seat (God's throne). Then *pride* set in. Satan decided that *he* wanted to *sit* on the throne. He wanted to *be* God, and so the controversy began, and Satan instantly became Gods number one enemy.

This happened in the first earth age.

We, the people, were all there in our spirit bodies (we have *two* bodies; we'll get into this later).

Satan was so good at deceiving the people that a third of God's children followed him and his evil ways.

We all had free will to choose *then* in our angelic bodies as we do now in our flesh bodies.

The one-third who followed Satan's deception amounted to approximately 3 billion people. Can you imagine that? We were *with* God. We could *see* God with our own eyes, yet so many would follow Satan. Astounding!

How could they be so taken in by him? Well, I've got a news flash for you. Many, many more follow Satan today than they did then, and when Satan returns to earth very soon (at the sixth trump) the whole world will whore after him. It is written that only *God's elect*, the ones who are in the know will *not* be deceived. Don't you want to stand with our Father?

He is definitely winning the *war of deception*. (Can you see now that deception is *truly* Satan's lethal weapon?)

People now in the flesh bodies still have free will to choose who to follow. God gave us the *gift* of free will.

So the controversy continues today. Look around at how evil engulfs the whole earth and is getting worse and worse as time passes. It is very important for people to learn God's Word so that they will *not* accept even any hint of deception.

Look at the false teachers and preachers and the lies of deception that they are spitting out. God told us long ago that this will happen. The lying preachers of deceptions are claiming to be sent by God but God tells us, "*I* never sent them." So if God didn't send them, they must be of Satan's group because they are certainly doing his work.

Use your gift of discernment and flee from all of these false preachers lest you be deceived yourselves. It's not too late but soon it *will* be. You *must* educate yourselves. This is my urgent message to you.

If this *book* can reach just one person, by instinct or discernment, who really wants to learn the truth and realize that God's truths do run deep, I will consider this book a *best seller*. It would be a work that did not fall on deaf ears but instead perked one's desires to learn the knowledge from God and to be a *true Christian*, and not just a person who simply *says* that he is one. (There is a huge difference between them, you know.) The end of this second earth age is quickly coming to an end.

Get into God's truth *now* because a person *can* wait one day too late. Don't be in that number. (You must close your flesh eyes to open your spiritual eyes. Go ahead, try it. You must also close your physical ears to be able to open your spiritual ears.)

The fifth trump is where we are *now* in time, and all prophecies are unfolding before our very eyes and *will* come to pass in this generation (the generation of the fig tree). This is the last generation. God loves us and is good to tell us this. Satan's return is at the sixth trump while we're still in the flesh, and it will last only five months (not three or five or seven years as is widely taught by lying nuts who call themselves preachers and teachers). While we're still in the flesh, Satan himself will be here, and he is bringing his whole bag of tricks with him. Be prepared!

God made it easy for us to recognize this sixth trump. At the end of that reign of power that God has allowed Satan for only five months, Christ will return at the seventh trump and, instantly, in the blink of an eye we are changed back into our spiritual bodies —and the Millennium begins. It is a one thousand-year time span to man but only one day in God's. It will be a time of teaching and a time of correction. All will be taught the straight truth (to those who did not have the opportunity to know truth) and, as it is written, many will *still* side with Satan and follow him to Hell to be blotted out forever and ever, never to be remembered by anyone again. (How sad this is!) Now, is it that difficult to believe God and to love Him? (I suppose it is to some.)

This is a testing time for us here on earth. God is testing us to see who we will choose, thus utilizing our free will. This really is what life is all about. It's entirely up for each individual to choose. Who do you choose? God or Satan?

God tells us that in these end times, in this generation, people will not hunger for bread but *will* hunger to hear the Word of God; and how true this is becoming. People are becoming fed up with religious nonsense. But they want to hear truth straight from God's own mouth.

That's the whole purpose of this book: To bring to you the whole truth from our Heavenly Father so that you will be aware of what God expects from us. God is not shy. He tells it like it is without beating around the bush.

He wants our love. He wants us to repent to Him so that He can erase all the bad stuff written by our name in the Book of Life. You can do this right now.

Always please God. Show him and prove to Him that you *care*, but be sincere about it. You can't trick Him; so don't try it.

God knows your *every thought* at all times day and night. Oh yes, He *can* and *does* read your mind 24–7. God never sleeps.

These truths are not open for debate. Truth is truth and lies are lies. It's just that simple. When God speaks, He leaves nothing half-said!

If the stuff that you are being taught does not coincide with God's Words, then you are being taken in by lies. Be very, very careful concerning the things that are being taught in your church. If what you are hearing and doing doesn't coincide with God's Word, then you are being taught man's made-up traditions, and you must get away and stay away from that stuff!

Your very soul—the most important and valuable asset that you have—can and most likely will end up being snuffed out by being sentenced to Hell! You *must* make that sincere change in your life's path to earn and achieve an eternal and unending home with God Himself. Let *God* be your destiny. It's the *only* destiny that you should want, for without God you have nothing.

What good is a person to God when he or she won't listen to Him?

If you will follow God, you *will* reap His wonderful truths and blessings. By choosing the evil path and Satan, you become totally worthless and useless to God. If you choose Satan, your destiny will be short-lived. Don't you want to live forever in an unending beautiful Heaven? Sure you do.

God made every person on earth for His pleasure. Read it for yourself in Revelation 4:11. "Thou art worthy, O Lord, to receive glory and honour and power: for thou hast created all things, and for thy pleasure they are and were created."

Please God. He loves you. He is your closest relative. He is our *only* true Father.

If you want to please Him, you instinctively would want as best you can to study His word, to show Him that you *do* care. God tells us to *study* to show yourself approved as it is written in 2 Timothy 2:15–16: "15Study to shew thyself approved unto God, a workman that needeth not to be ashamed, rightly dividing the word of truth. [16]But shun profane and vain babblings: for they will increase unto more ungodliness."

So do it.

To just truthfully and sincerely *try*, you will be counted as *perfect* by our Heavenly Father. God is very fair.

Ignorance of God's Word will "hold no water" when you stand face-to-face before God at the Great White Throne Judgment. It won't matter about what some man said. If it isn't God's truth, it doesn't count.

It's no different today in the courts of our land. If you claim before a court that you didn't know about the existence of a certain law, you'll quickly be told that *ignorance* is not a valid defense. Ignorance does *not* count.

God is not different. All people need to educate themselves, as best as they possibly can, about God's truths, wishes, wants, and demands. If you intend to inherit God's awesome creation of a never-ending Heaven, then it becomes a *must* for you to "study to show yourself approved."

It is God's direct demand to us!

So do it. Study! Please our Father.

Amen.

Flush all the false stuff out of your mind and totally and completely replace it with God's Word.

6. How do I learn and where do I start? Jesus describes it best. In the beginning of your studies, you must start out with the *milk* of God's Word and slowly graduate to the *meat* of His Word. This book is written to start you out in the *milk* of God's Word and to ease you into the *meat* that he instructs you to learn in the end. The *meat* is simply a deeper study into the entirety of His word and to gradually learn the profound meanings of His Holy Word. Everyone has their very own appetite for learning, and God

knows that. Just a *sincere* small appetite goes a very long way with our Father. (The key words here are *sincere appetite*). Don't try to fool Him because He knows whether you are actually sincere. He knows *everything*, and mankind knows very little! You can possess all the academic degrees that cover an entire wall but they are worthless when compared to God. You could have tons of money but it's worthless to Him. All the success in this journey through life are worthless *if* you don't "first seek the kingdom of God." You must study to "show yourselves approved." If you don't do that, you put yourself in grave danger of losing your soul at the Great White Throne Judgment at the end of the quickly approaching Millennium Age.

You can believe this or not; God's truths are "cut and dried." God has foretold us all things and it's our job to *learn* all these. Have you been taught that you need to give your soul to God? Well you've been lied to.

God says, "I own all souls." He can do whatever He wants to do with them. He can give them an everlasting and eternal life, or He can send them to the destructive Hell that awaits those who choose the wrong path by not including God in the equation of their everyday lives. Every one will get everything they have earned and deserve all at one time. What do you deserve?

7. *Satan and his spiritual powers* are allowed to roam this earth, and God is allowing this to happen.

This is a testing time to see who, out of all His children, will decide to follow Satan when he sits in Jerusalem *claiming* to be the "real" Jesus Christ.

People will easily be fooled because they have not been taught the dire importance of this factual truth.

So the question is, which one will you choose? Will you choose the true one or the evil one?

Satan, the first one arriving, comes in so peacefully saying, "Come follow me and I'll give you anything you ask for, and I'll give it to you in abundance because I love you and I've come to save you; simply love and worship *me* and that is all I require of you." (It is as if he is saying, "Do you want riches? Here, take these sacks full of money. Want a big fancy house with a five-car garage? Okay I'll give you that, and here let me give you this thirty-six-foot yacht to go along with it. Just love and worship me and that's all I want in return. Are you into dope and so forth? Here, let me give you two twenty-five-pound bags of the very best cocaine ever made. Oh, one other thing, do you remember that beautiful woman you saw on TV the other day? Well, I'm giving her to you too. Just love and follow me always because I'm Jesus Christ and I love you dearly. Tell your friends to get in line, and I'll also grant them all their wishes and desires. Tell them how much I love them—hurry. Tell them to come to me, and we'll talk because I have a whole bunch of promises for *all* the people around this beautiful world that I created with these two hands; and I did it all by myself. I am great. I am your Savior. I want your love, that's all. Come one, come all.")

Well, now that was quite an example, wasn't it?

You need to learn *truth* and quit following man's "wild imagination" concerning the rapture and many other disgusting lies that is spewed out to the assembly of followers.

Get yourself an excellent education in God's Word or get out from behind your pulpit and keep your lying lips shut.

I despise lying preachers, but what's much more important is *God* hates lying preachers. If you don't know what you're talking about and mislead your people, you *are* and *will be* held responsible for the demise of these mislead souls.

You, false preachers, are accountable for your own teachings.

If you cannot teach *truth and truth only*, then you need to change professions. Quickly!

Go drive a truck or be a politician; yes be a politician, they blow hot air too. And you will feel "right at home!"

Here are a few scriptures that God wants you to learn, which He Himself is speaking:

6My people are destroyed for lack of knowledge: because thou hast rejected knowledge, I will also reject thee, that thou shalt be no priest to me: seeing thou hast forgotten the law of thy God, I will also forget thy children. (Hosea 4:6)

9Who is wise, and he shall understand these things? prudent, and he shall know them? for the ways of the Lord are right, and the just shall walk in them: but the transgressors shall fall therein [through deception]. (Hosea 14:9)

4He that saith, I know him, and keepeth not his commandments, is a liar, and the truth is not in him. (1 John 2:4)

10And with all deceivableness of unrighteousness in them that perish; because they received not the love of the truth, that they might be saved. 11And for this cause God shall send them strong delusion, that they should believe a lie: 12That they all might be damned who believed not the truth, but had pleasure in unrighteousness. (2 Thessalonians 2:10–12)

[Here Isaiah writes to show that people want truth, not lies. It's instinct.] 8It shall even be as when an hungry man dreameth, and, behold, he eateth; but he awaketh, and his soul is empty: or as when a thirsty man dreameth, and, behold, he drinketh; but he awaketh, and, behold, he is faint, and his soul hath appetite: so shall the multitude of all the nations be, that fight against mount Zion. (Isaiah 29:8)

11Behold, the days come, saith the Lord GOD, that I will send a famine in the land, not a famine of bread, nor a thirst for water, but of hearing the words of the Lord. (Amos 8:11)

This famine is upon us now. People need and are searching for truth, not food. God just said it. So what do we do?

It's quite simple: we search out *the truth in God's Word* instead of listening to "fairy tales" because deception runs rampant in *most* of the so-called churches.

Be ever so careful about the things you listen to.

Be able to ask questions to your local pastor and weigh his answers carefully. Check him out in "what God saith."

Discern whether you are being taught truth, and if you should find that you are being deceived by lies then get out of there!

I promise you that it is *not* a church that God approves of. They simply are "calling themselves a church."

If a so-called pastor can't back up his teachings and document his statements with God's Word, then he should not be there in his pulpit beating his gums. Warning: Be *very, very, very* careful of *who* and *what* you listen to. God warns us over and over: Beware of false teachers and preachers that come in "my name" claiming that they have been sent by God, but God says, "I never knew them." If you listen to a fool you become a bigger fool than they are!

What does God's word say about a *fool?*

> 26He that trusteth in his own heart is a fool: but whoso walketh wisely, he shall be delivered. (Proverbs 28:26)

> 12The words of a wise man's mouth are gracious; but the lips of a fool will swallow up himself. (Ecclesiastes 10:12)

> 11As the partridge sitteth on eggs, and hatcheth them not; so he that getteth riches, and not by right, shall leave them in the midst of his days, and at his end shall be a fool. (Jeremiah 17:11)

> 14A fool also is full of words: a man cannot tell what shall be; [Because of the foolish words] and what shall be after him, who can tell him? [He babbles on and on lies, lies, lies.] (Ecclesiastes 10:14)

Now it's time for God to tell us what He thinks about *false prophets, preachers and teachers.* (Those who claim to be sent by

God and/or those standing in church spewing out lies concerning God's truths.)

> [11]And many false prophets [preachers, teachers not sent by God] shall rise, and shall deceive many. (Matthew 24:11)

> [15]Beware of false prophets, which come to you in sheep's clothing, but inwardly they are ravening wolves. (Matthew 7:15)

> [24]For there shall arise false Christs [preachers, teachers] and false prophets, and shall shew great signs and wonders; insomuch that, if it were possible, they shall deceive the very elect. (Matthew 24:24)

> [26]Woe unto you, [false preachers] when all men shall speak well of you! for so did their fathers to the false prophets. (Luke 6:26)

> [13]For such are false apostles, deceitful workers, transforming themselves into the apostles of Christ. [14]And no marvel; for Satan himself is transformed into an angel of light [acting as, claiming to be Jesus Christ]. [15]Therefore it is no great thing if his ministers [Satan's so-called preachers] also be transformed as the ministers of righteousness; whose end shall be according to their works [preachers that lie and mislead their flocks]. (2 Corinthians 11:13–15)

> [1]But there were false prophets also among the people, even as there shall be false teachers among you, who privily shall bring in damnable heresies, even denying the Lord that bought them, and bring upon themselves swift destruction [and to those who believe their lies]. (2 Peter 2:1)

> [1]Beloved, believe not every spirit, but try the spirits whether they are of God: because many false prophets are gone out into the world [use the gift of discernment that God gave us all]. (1 John 4:1)

These lying deceivers are supergood. They are, in most churches today, posing as pastors, youth pastors, Sunday school teachers, elders, deacons, etc. I've known many deacons that absolutely know almost nothing about God's Word. I, too, believe that most teach lies simply out of ignorance of God's Word. They may *think* they know the truth, but they really don't. The dangers lie with the fact that these teachers/preachers are passing on, from generation to generation, man's doctrines and religions that they've been taught. They may think that everything that they've been taught is the "gospel truth," but if they cannot back it up with scripture from God's Word, they are lying, maybe not on purpose but simply, out of ignorance.

This is why *you* need to educate yourself in *truth* so that you can utilize the *gift of discernment* given to us by our Heavenly Father. He is so very good to us, and we all should seek to possess the knowledge that God offers to us.

Guess what, it's totally free. It's ours for the taking. How much more loving can our Father be?

So, study to "show yourself approved" and never ever fill your head with the junk of "man's imaginations" and "dreams" of grandeur that come with false teachings, or you *will* be sucked-in by Satan himself and end up with your brain (your head) crammed full of the mark of the beast.

That's what the mark is—the lies of man's traditions—the twisting of the truth by liars that you've filled your mind with.

Pretend your mind is a toilet, full of falseness. Simply "flush it!" Satan's return is very, very near. The sands of time is close to running out. Time is wasting away. Get busy. Study, study, study; learn, learn, and learn. God prophesies in Matthew 24:34–36: "[34]Verily I say unto you, This generation shall not pass, till all these things be fulfilled. [35]Heaven and earth shall pass away, but my words shall not pass away. [36]But of that day and hour knoweth no man, no, not the angels of heaven, but my Father only."

In verse 34, the generation that God is mentioning is called the "generation of the fig tree."

Ever heard of it?

Ever been taught anything about it?

It is so important that you learn all about this, the last generation.

You must learn about and believe it because God has told us all about it in both the Old and the New Testaments.

(We'll get into the "meat" of this generational prophecy in volume II, assuming that God will permit me enough time to get it published before I pass away back to Him.)

In the meantime, I want you to ask your pastor to make "the generation of the fig tree" the topic in his next sermon. Ask him to teach the congregation all about it and why *that knowledge* is so specifically important to us today.

Test him. See what he's got to say. You may find that he's "on top of his game" or you may find that he doesn't know anything at all about it. Today's seminaries need to teach their students about the generation of the fig tree. Why? Because we are now in this generation.

Ask him to teach all of you about the seven trumps and what happens in each one of them.

The *trumps* are simply a timetable of events that we must know.

Ask your pastor about Satan and his return and how long he has on earth when he comes.

Ask him why he teaches the rapture.

Ask him to teach you in detail all about it! You may be amazed at his answer! You may find that he has "no meat" of God's Word to offer you, and you may find that he needs more "milk" himself. I don't know, but find out for yourself. You may marvel at his answers!

You must possess wisdom because God *is* wisdom. Do you want wisdom?

My sincere advice to all of you is to better learn all about God's wisdom! You need to be wise also. All wisdom comes from God.

You better "get with the program" and discipline yourself to learning God's Word. Time is running out!

You must study daily! On a daily schedule, go into the *closet* of your mind and feed it with pure unadulterated *truth*. Learn God's *truth*, not "man's traditions." "Man's traditions" make Gods word null and void.

Now if you don't *try* your very best—the key word being *try*—to study and retain His truths, you *will* face major embarrassment on that day of judgment. It's all up to you, it's your choice on how you wish to be judged. Judgment can be a good thing. You could hear from Him the words "A job well done" or "And receive your rewards." You also could hear from Him "Why didn't you learn my word?," "What use are you to me?," "Why should I save *you* from the pit?," "You didn't care enough about me to study my instructions that I sent to you. You didn't even care *just a little bit* about my Holy Scripture," "You never did open my letters, the Bible, to see the wonderful, majestic, and magnificent wonders that I have created for my people—the 'tried and true.'"

The ones of those who truly love Him realize the things that He expects of them while in the flesh. Now how could you possibly convince Him of your love for Him if you never studied His word?

You couldn't. He sees all. He knows all. He is a heart knower. He is a mind knower and that's why you can't pull the wool over His eyes (you can't fool Him). God is supernatural.

It is very rare that I meet anyone who can discuss God's Word with me, and I find this shameful.

They look at me like they are in never-never land. They draw a complete blank. Why? Because they haven't been taught truth.

Almost all are wearing that "cloak of security" that their particular denomination offers. They, no doubt, feel that they are heaven bound. They may find it to be a false cloak.

It's what they've been taught. They do not understand that a "church" or a "denomination" cannot save them and neither can any man. It's a one-on-one with God that gets the job done. There is *no* other way.

People say, "I just listen to my pastor and am happy with all he has to say and teach me." Oh really? Surely you don't think that he can give you a "ticket to Heaven." Actually denominational teachings and beliefs—almost all every time—will issue you a "ticket to Hell" as a result of false teachings!

Most denominations are most likely the work of Satan, and mankind doesn't realize it.

Talk about being duped!

Why do I say that?

Well, listen to me closely. All denominations believe differently: the Catholics have their beliefs and rituals, the Baptists likewise do too, the Church of Christ, the Methodist Church, the Lutheran Church, the Jehovah's Witnesses, and oh, let's not forget the Muslims and their different offshoots, the Buddhists, the atheists, and hundreds of sects and on and on it goes—confusion, confusion, confusion.

So the question is, "Which one of these religions can you truly believe in?"

They all think and practice differently, believing that *their* "religion" is *the only true religion.*

What's wrong with this picture? Come on now, think about this. Think deeply.

God hates denominations. Why? Because the word itself means division; it is a division of beliefs. It is a division of God's Word, thus a *twist* of God's Word.

These divisions create *false teachings* every time.

News flash: the score is 47 to 3. It's the fourth quarter and Satan is well ahead. It's going to take a huge comeback for us to win, and we *will* win but with a lot fewer players. Which side are you *really* playing on?

In the beginning of this second earth age in the flesh, God wanted to be our King, *the one and only King*, but we His children rebelled and demanded a "king" whom we could visually see. And so denominations sprang forth by the hundreds, and the rest is history.

Wake up! Come out of confusion! God says we are *rebellious and stubborn*, but we don't have to stay that way!

In Psalms 78:7–8, God says, "⁷That they might set their hope in God, and not forget the works of God, but keep his commandments: ⁸And might not be as their fathers, a stubborn and rebellious generation; a generation that set not their heart aright, and whose spirit was not stedfast with God." And in 2 Timothy 2:15–16: "*¹⁵Study to shew thyself approved unto God, a workman that needeth not to be ashamed, rightly dividing the word of truth. ¹⁶But shun profane and vain babblings: for they will increase unto more ungodliness.*"

We must *shun* liars who change the actual and true word of God and twist these truths to fit their own agenda. Avoid such falseness.

God says in 2 Timothy 2:20–21, "²⁰But in a great house there are not only vessels of gold and of silver, but also of wood and of earth; and some to honour, and some to dishonour. ²¹If a man therefore purge himself from these, he shall be a vessel unto honour, sanctified, and meet for the master's use, and prepared unto every good work."

Do we want to be of use to God? Of course we do! Let's all strive to meet that goal. We *will* be winners!

It's quite simple.

Follow these scriptures to a tee. *Believe* Gods' word. *Honor* and *follow* it and avoid the babblings that are running rampant today. Babble means confusion.

In my lifetime, I have never seen and heard more phony preachers that we have on television today, and what's even worse is people believe and support these lying screwballs by sending them their hard-earned bucks so that they can get "blessings and healings." Oh, how stupid can one person be? Ignorance runs rampant! (Never send these liars money!)

God will give you *true* blessings and healings and is absolutely— *free*! Trust in God, He'll never leave us nor forsake us.

As I mentioned before, do not support these idiots that claim "to be of God." Many are doing Satan's work and, trust me, some know beyond any shadow of doubt that Satan is their father. They know that they are lying to you. Don't fall for their lies and falseness.

Listen. Their lies have created a multibillion dollar "healing" industry. They don't care about you and your soul's ultimate demise, but they *do* want your money! And that is *all* they want.

Do you know what a hypocrite is? It's a play actor. And boy, they can act!

They are as a thorn in God's eye, and the "cup of wrath" that Christ is bringing with Him at His return will be poured out right on top of their heads, and yours, too, if you have supported these nuts (play actors). Don't be a fool! They are a bunch of phonies.

The power of God is awesome! His power is so awesome that we, in the flesh, cannot even begin to conceive His majestic wonders because they run *ever so deep*, but we will be brought to *full remembrance* at Christ's return. Let's simply be patient; do things God's way and watch for Satan's coming when he is claiming to be Christ at the sixth trump; but five months later, our *true* Savior will be here—the seventh trump.

God's Word states: "²⁶But the Comforter, which is the Holy Spirit, whom the Father will send in my name, he shall teach you all things, and bring all things to your remembrance, whatsoever I have said unto you" (John 14:26). (Always replace the word *ghost* with *spirit*. God is not a spook!) "⁵I will therefore put you in remembrance, though ye once knew this, how that the Lord, having saved the people out of the land of Egypt, afterward destroyed them that believed not" (Jude 1:5).

In 2 Peter 1:12–13, 15 we read:

> ¹²Wherefore I will not be negligent to put you always in remembrance of these things, though ye know them, and be established in the present truth. ¹³Yea, I think it meet, as long as I am in this tabernacle, to stir you up by putting

you in remembrance; [15]Moreover I will endeavour that ye may be able after my decease to have these things always in remembrance.

And 1 Timothy 4:6, 7 states "[6]If thou put the brethren in remembrance of these things, thou shalt be a good minister of Jesus Christ, nourished up in the words of faith and of good doctrine, whereunto thou hast attained. [7]But refuse profane and old wives' fables, and exercise thyself rather unto godliness."

Faith? What is faith? (Do *you* have faith? Are you sure?)

Here is the definition and two examples of true faith in Hebrews 11:1, 6, 7:

> [1]Now faith is the substance of things hoped for, the evidence of things not seen. [6]But without faith it is impossible to please him: for he that cometh to God must believe that he is, and that he is a rewarder of them that diligently seek him. [7]By faith Noah, being warned of God of things not seen as yet, moved with fear, [reverence and love] prepared an ark to the saving of his house; by the which he condemned the world, and became heir of the righteousness which is by faith.

This chapter of Hebrews gives you an exact account of our forefathers' faith. I urge you to read it. Read it over and over and give it deep thought.

Gain *faith* for "*without faith, it is impossible to please God.*"

Start right now and learn to have *faith* in our living Father. Don't wait until it is "one day too late." Anyone of us could drop dead at any moment. Be prepared to face judgment. You can have *faith* that Judgment Day isn't far off. Let's get prepared now!

Don't wait until it is one day too late!

THE RAPTURE

Surely no one believes in such nonsense as *the rapture*, but sadly there are those who do! God detests those who teach this false event and the believers also.

Let's start directly with scripture from our Heavenly Father. Would you prefer listening to Him or would you rather prefer to some windbag?

Pay close attention to God's words at what He says in Ezekiel 13:2–3, 5–6, 9, 20–21:

> ²Son of man, prophesy [teach] against the prophets [preachers] of Israel [we, the United States of America is in most part the house of Israel] that prophesy, and say thou unto them that prophesy out of their own hearts [minds] Hear ye the word of the LORD; ³Thus saith the Lord GOD; Woe unto the foolish prophets [preachers] that follow their own spirit [not God's spirit] and have seen nothing! [God is very emphatic in this verse.] ⁵Ye have not gone up into the gaps, neither made up the hedge for the house of Israel to stand [not fly] in the battle in the day of the LORD. [A coward flies off, but a true man of God stands with the Lord.] ⁶They have seen vanity and lying divination [these so-called church preachers dream stuff up and the people go for it] saying, The LORD saith: [and the Lord did not say it] and the LORD hath not sent them: [these preachers are not sent by me, the Lord saying] and they have made *others* to hope that they would confirm the word. [These lying preachers are not "confirmed" in God's Word, and our Father has a very special place prepared for these screwballs. It's called "the Lake of Fire" and God Himself is the consuming fire. What does a fire do? Answer: It makes stuff extinct! Want to be extinct?] ⁹And mine hand shall be upon the prophets [the lying preachers spreading this dreamed up "rapture Bologny"] that see vanity [empty words with not truth in them] and that divine lies: they shall not be in

the assembly of my people [those that stand with me and not fly off into la-la land teachings] neither shall they be written in the writing [the book of life] of the house of Israel, neither shall they enter into the land of Israel; and ye shall know that I *am (God's Holy name)* the Lord GOD. [Yes, these phony, lying preachers are, very soon going to have a very sad awakening! Now, imagine for a moment God has his hands reaching out to His children so that they will come to Him and learn *His truth from His very own lips*. But these lying preachers, men and/or women, are getting in the way of His "true salvation" by cramming people's minds full of lies, and our Father *hates* this rapture teaching of "*flying* to save your soul." God is coming *here* to earth. Heaven will be *here* on this earth, so where do you think you are going to fly off to? God wants us to *stand* with Him to show Him that we love Him and that we *want* to take *that stand*.] ²⁰Wherefore thus saith the Lord GOD; Behold, I *am* against your pillows [that you throw over my hands so that people can't see truth] wherewith ye there hunt the souls to make *them* fly, and I will tear them from your arms, and will let the souls go, *even* the souls that ye hunt to make *them* fly. ²¹Your kerchiefs also will I tear, and deliver my people out of your hand, and they shall be no more in your hand to be hunted; and ye shall know that I *am (God's Holy name)* the LORD.

God further says in Ezekiel 12:25, "²⁵For I *am* the LORD: I will speak, and the word that I shall speak shall come to pass; it shall be no more prolonged: for in your days, O rebellious house, will I say the word, and will perform it, saith the Lord GOD" and Ephesians 6:11 to "¹¹Put on the whole armour of God, that ye may be able to stand against the wiles of the devil."

The "armor" is God's truths, the whole truth. He expects us to absorb that truth so that we can stand with Him in the upcoming appearance and arrival of Satan himself at the sixth trump.

Satan's message will be that "I've come to fly you out of here, so come one, come all."

If you believe in this false rapture stuff, then you'll be "easy pickings" for him, and that creates a huge problem for you rapture believers because you'll be taken by Satan. Do you get it? You don't want to fly off with Satan, do you?

Since the rapture teachings are of Satan, they therefore are false. Those lies in no way whatsoever align with God's true word. As you can see, the teaching is exactly the *opposite* of God's Word.

If you still want to believe in the rapture after this proof that I have given you, then God has yet another warning for you!

God says in 2 Thessalonians 2:10–12: "¹⁰And with all deceivableness of unrighteousness in them that perish; because they received not the love of the truth, that they might be saved. ¹¹And for this cause God shall send them strong delusion, that they should believe a lie: ¹²That they all might be damned who believed not the truth, but had pleasure in unrighteousness."

These "strong delusions" are designed by God for the hardheads who won't listen. God's Word is meant to *buildup* not to teardown. Believe me you do not want to live in a "state of delusion," do you?

Wake up! Get yourselves away from this false teaching.

Flush it away from your mind. It is one *big* lie!

Better yet, give this book to your preacher!

IS THE BIBLE TRUE?

To doubt the written word of God is a very unwise and dangerous thing to do! *Never* doubt *any* of His word.

History itself proves God's Word to be factual. The Chinese have always been fantastic record-keepers, and Noah's flood is noted by their scholars plus many other events that are written in the Bible.

My favorite example to use as proof is Psalms 22, which was penned by David.

History alone proves that it was written one thousand years before Christ was crucified, and everyone knows that history cannot be altered. Why? Because a fact is a fact!

Psalms 22 was prophecy when it was written. This chapter describes in detail Christ's own words that He would speak while nailed to that cross. And one thousand years later at Christ's Crucifixion, it came to pass exactly as it was written.

Christ quoted it as He suffered on that cross. Why? He wanted us to know, beyond any doubt, that not only *this* prophecy, but *all* written prophecies in the Bible are absolutely true.

Who, besides God himself, could write, through David, with such accurate accounting? Answer: No one.

It's important that you read all thirty-one verses in that twenty-second chapter of Psalms. It will amaze you!

For more proof, turn to Matthew 27 and Mark 15 and read the Crucifixion again keeping in mind that one thousand-year span of time.

God's truth cannot be denied. God wrote no fairy tales. When He tells us facts, there is no room for doubt. Truth is truth!

It seems that some people try to disprove God's sacred word, but they run into a brick wall every time.

However *proving* God's Word is simple and easy.

Disapproving God's Word is impossible. It's a waste of time.

God says in 1 Corinthians 15:58: "[58]Therefore, my beloved brethren, be ye stedfast, unmoveable, always abounding in the work of the Lord, forasmuch as ye know that your labour is not in vain in the Lord."

You must always be *steadfast* in truth and keep His truth close to your heart. Keep it foremost in your mind.

Some things must be accepted as fact whether you like it or not.

Yes, the Bible is true. Every word in it is truth directly from God's own lips; and *God cannot lie.* Even God's name is a fact! *Cherish it!* He *is* our Father.

"*I Am That I Am*"

What, you may ask, does "I am that I am" mean? Answer: It means "I am that I am."

Get it? It's fact, not fiction!

Facts have to be accepted at face value.

6

THE MARK OF THE BEAST

The *mark of the beast* has been noted to be the most dreaded mark that a person can have. So here is *truth*.

People have been led to believe that they will be branded by Satan with 666 across their forehead or a tattoo here or a tattoo there or some other mark somewhere on their bodies. That is another false teaching that only those who are gullible would believe. It's a silly belief!

The mark of the beast is *not* something planted on your body. It is something planted inside your body—*your brain*.

All the mark means is that you've been impregnated with false teachings and false information. It means that you've been lied to and that you have believed those lies and stuck to them—and that is bad, bad, bad. But guess what, Satan is happy to have you in his camp!

You probably have not been taught that Satan comes back to earth in person at the sixth trump claiming to be God, but he is actually the *instead of god*. Did you know that? (He is actually the Antichrist, the *instead of Christ*!)

Have you ever heard someone say that they want to be the *first taken* (upon his arrival)? Have you heard (and *believed*) that false teaching? Satan will be the one taking you, not God.

Do you believe in the rapture? There is *no* rapture. Our true Christ returns at the seventh trump, not the sixth trump (you must never forget this!). Why has your pastor not told you of these facts? It's the main theme of the Bible—deception. It's Satan's lethal weapon!

If you believe in the rapture, *you do have the mark of the beast.*

If you believe that you want to be the *first taken* and follow through with your belief, *you do have the mark of the beast.*

If you are not aware that Satan arrives here at the sixth trump claiming to be Jesus, then *you do have the mark of the beast.*

You can erase that mark in your brain by learning the truth. The truth comes to us straight from God's lips.

If you've been taught these lies at your church, then you don't need to waste your time there. Find a church that doesn't lie to its congregation. God gave us all discernment, so use it.

Do not be deceived. Deception is Satan's most lethal weapon. Do not get caught up in his web of lies.

God's truth is here for the taking, so take it! (Educate yourselves in truth instead of fairy tales; that is, if you want to achieve Heaven instead of Hell!)

So rid yourself of the mark of the beast. You need to know that Satan returns to this earth claiming to be Jesus Christ, our real Jesus Christ. It's a lie, don't fall for it. He's a fake.

God has allowed Satan many alluring powers of persuasion to fool you into believing his (Satan's) lies.

Why would God do that? Answer: To *test* you! God wants to know if you've done your homework. God wants to know if you give a flip one way or the other.

So prepare yourselves because the *big test* is going to happen in this, the last generation.

THE THREE EARTH AGES

If a person doesn't understand the beginning, he in no way can understand the end. So let's talk a little about *time*, that is, God's time.

We read in 2 Peter 3:8, "⁸But, beloved, be not ignorant of this one thing, that one day is with the Lord as a thousand years, and a thousand years as one day."

This verse is necessary for you to understand. This verse is simply stating that one thousand years in *man's time* equals only one day in *God's time*. Now we can better understand why this one day is referred to as *the Lord's Day* all throughout the Bible. Ignorant preachers most often say the Lord's Day is Sunday, a day of the week. But the Lord's Day is the Millennium (one thousand years).

The First Earth Age

The first earth age is well documented in the Bible as well as in science itself.

Prehistoric relics, bones of all sorts of beasts, etc. are continually being unearthed, and through modern-day technology such as the use of carbon dating and other methods, a time line concerning the estimated age of these many creatures' remains can be determined.

As a result, we know as of years ago—there is no argument among the experts—that this all came about in the first earth age.

Everyone should forget this big bang theory stuff and come back down to reality and accept the fact that God is in charge and everything He does is perfect. He has unimaginable powers that are so far above mankind's knowledge and thinking abilities that we will never solve most scientific mysteries to their fullest! The so-called experts will solve only the mysteries that God intends for us to know. But when it is time, God will reveal all in His time.

(There is not a doubt that God has to have a great sense of humor as He looks down at His creation of mankind that He so carefully created.) Most people don't appreciate His powers involved in creating this beautiful planet earth with everything in it! He even created the air we breathe.

Who can make air? Do you think it "just happened?"

Who can create water? Who can create life? Can the experts create dirt? Do you believe that God even exists? Many do, many don't.

Many people will not accept the fact that God created everything. Why did He create every single thing that exists?

In Revelation 4:11 God says, "*¹¹Thou art worthy, O Lord, to receive glory and honour and power: for thou hast created all things, and for thy pleasure they are and were created.*"

Have you pleased Him lately? Have you told Him lately that you love Him?

Can you imagine the billions of dollars that has been and is being spent by these so-called experts, trying to figure out how this or that came to be or even why it exists?

Some even claim evolution created man as he appears today (mankind's ignorance, both of the past and present, is an amazing thing), but one thing is for sure, He did not create *ignorance* for His pleasure! (But ignorance of God's Word *will* buy you a *ticket to Hell* though. Do you want that? Do you want to believe that left-wing ideology for a ticket to Hell?)

Oh, the nutty professors out there spreading their "words of wisdom" are yet another amazing thing. People should be ashamed of themselves for even listening to and/or reading such man-made nonsense. It's stupidity at its max! (This stuff is ruining the minds of our young men and women.)

The so-called brains of the world should use those *sheep skins* to start a good campfire and go back to school! To God's school!

(Learn something of *real* value and earn yourselves a *secured ticket to Heaven.*)

Ignorance of God's Word is as a *thorn in God's eyes.* Those idiots, the left-wing nuts, are an irritation to Him. Idiots create more idiots (trash in, trash out). Ignorance is as smoke in God's nostrils. (Ever had smoke in your nostrils?) The day will come that all knees will bow before God and be judged according to our works here on earth. (Your work is all that you can take with you when you die.) At that time, we will realize how insignificant our existence was here on earth compared to God's majesty. You'll see the *real truth* (for God is truth) as you look at Him face-to-face, one-on-one. Will you left wingers spew out your great theories of your so-called wisdom when this Great White Throne Judgment Day comes to fruition? Answer: *No,* you won't! You'll feel about as significant as a gnat! (So wake up and smell the roses! God does *not* deal in theories, *He deals in facts* and *only* facts. And *that's* a fact!)

God says in 1 Peter 1:17, "[17]And if ye call on the Father, who without respect of persons judgeth according to every man's work, pass the time of your sojourning here in fear [fear means reverence]" and in Revelation 22:12, "[12]And, behold, I come quickly; and my reward is with me, to give every man according as his work shall be [Your clothes will be woven according to your good and faithful works; no work, no clothing! It may not be a pretty sight to see you naked!]."

Now back to the first earth age.

I went to great lengths here to show you that our time here in these flesh bodies is but a couple of hours compared to *God's time.* How we use this gift of time of only two hours is what *life* is all about. It is of importance to please our Heavenly Father, so we *must* wisely spend our time learning *truth* and *truth* only.

It is reality. This is why I say to you that true Christianity is not a religion, it's reality; so stay with me here and learn.

Get all that religious stuff that you've been taught out of your mind. Flush it out! That is why God hates "religions." They all preach and teach their different and insignificant "stuff." So you don't need "that old time religion" and you don't need a church because I assure you, there is *no* religion *nor* any church that can save you! *None* and I mean *none* can save you. Only God can. You must confess your sins *directly* to our Father (never go through a "middle man"). If you think you have to, then you have been lied to. It's hogwash! True hogwash!

Don't you realize the reason that God created the Millennium, which is coming shortly, is to give the unlearned the *opportunity* to learn truth? *He knows* all about the lies of deception that are being taught in these so-called churches and all of man's "holy rituals" they perform. These things hurt Him deeply. They hurt Him to tears, and I feel the great sorrow with Him. I see it and I understand it. It's sad.

There are no *second chances*. But with the lies that are being taught today to the people, they have had *no chance* of hearing and learning the in-depth truths of God's Word; but you'll have that chance in the Millennium (the *true Lord's Day*).

Can you imagine being taught by God (and His elect) in person? How wonderful!

But guess what, many will *still* remain stiff-necked and *refuse* God's Word. So what's new? My, my, my! Man and his stupid infinite wisdom!

So let's cut to the chase, you either *believe in and do* God's work or you don't. (Is Heaven in your plans or does Hell really suit your fancy?)

Only God can give you His blessings. No man can. If you think otherwise, you have spent your time here on God's earth listening to lies and have become caught up in fake rituals performed by fake preachers, pastors, priests, teachers, rabbis, or whatever title they claim to have, or whatever name they wish to be called by. You've been had! (Give this a deep personal thought.)

I know that most of you think I'm talking like some of kind of religious fanatic. That's okay if you do. Christ taught the same thing because He did not want you to be deceived. He warned us all about the fact that deceptive preachers would come *claiming* to be "men of God" spreading lies of deceit. What did the people do to Christ for teaching truth, and only truth? They killed Him! (They shamed and mocked Him! They spat upon Him! They pierced Him. They drove spikes through His hands and feet and laughed at Him.)

Payback time is just around the corner, and Christ will be coming back here. Are you prepared? Got all your ducks in order? Are you *deceived*? If you are, you are truly stupid! If you have *true faith* and knowledge and love for our Creator (our Father) then He'll take no vengeance toward you. He loves you. He's your next of kin. He's your Father (your Dad).

God is totally fair the same as we try to be with our own offspring, but some of us will have the one in our family that we have to chastise time and time again; sometimes to the point of having to set them aside or even of disowning him or her. God is no different. Do you want to be set aside and become a reject?

During the first earth age, we were all in our angelic bodies. We looked then as we do now. We all appeared to be about thirty years old. We had mass. We were not some Casper the ghost with wings flittering here and there and sitting on some soft cloud up in the sky. We were God's creation in our angelic bodies, and we roamed the earth just as we do today.

We had free will then in the first earth age, as we have here in the flesh today in this second earth age. Satan was there too, and like today he set out to deceive as many souls as he could. He was a deceiver then, and he is a deceiver now.

He wanted the angelic bodied creatures (people we'll call them) to follow him as he wants us to follow him today. He uses every deceptive thing he can conjure up. He knows every man's weakness and uses it to his advantage to entice people over to his side.

By using his way of thinking, including flattery, in that first earth age, he managed to convince about one-third of the people, God's beautiful creation, over to his side, and so the *great controversy began*; the bad versus the good, the truth versus the lies (just as it is today).

Now since this one-third chose to deny God and worship Satan, God decided that instead of killing them He would do something else. So He looked toward them and said, "Let's make man in our own image. Let's make mankind to look just like we are." And so we do. God loves His children and to kill one-third (about four billion) of them would have crushed Him. How would we feel if we had to kill even one of *our* children?

Considering that one-half (six billion) of God's children have already passed away and the other half (six to seven billion) is alive today, we can come pretty close by estimating that God created twelve to thirteen billion children. It isn't written or recorded in the Bible, but it is a good estimation.

I want you to recall what I just told you that Satan was, as we all were, there in the first earth age, and he caused much trouble; and that a great rebellion among God's children came about resulting in God's creation of the second earth age for mankind as we are today.

At the end of this first earth age, God grieved greatly about our rebellion against Him. The same rebellion has come full circle and is upon us again. (What goes around, comes around. It seems like we never seem to learn.)

God says in Jeremiah 4:14, 22, 26–27,

> ¹⁴O Jerusalem, wash thine heart from wickedness, that thou mayest be saved. How long shall thy vain thoughts lodge within thee? ²²For my people is foolish, they have not known me; they are sottish children, and they have none understanding: they are wise to do evil, but to do

good they have no knowledge. [Because so many of God's children chose Satan over Him, His anger erupted. Erupted big time! Then what happened?] 26I beheld, and, lo, the fruitful place was a wilderness, and all the cities thereof were broken down at the presence of the LORD, and by his fierce anger. [Notice that we had cities then too, and God 'cleaned house' by destroying them all; and guess what, He is going to do it again at His return. Why? Because mankind is rebelling again and, as a whole, couldn't care less about Him.] 27For thus hath the LORD said, The whole land shall be desolate; yet will I not make a full end. [So our Father ended that first earth age.]

Much, much more can be written and is written about the first earth age—and even before—but for now we'll move on.

The Second Earth Age

As the second earth age begins about eight thousand years ago, so mankind begins also.

God wanted us to be conceived in the womb and to be born of the water, inside the womb, in the flesh, and He places our souls (our real selves) inside these flesh bodies at conception. We all have been created the same, our flesh bodies having our very own souls inside. Your soul is the *real* you. God made you and, therefore, owns you and your soul as well.

(Oh, by the way, have you noticed? We have no wings! This is yet another false imagination of man. Oh, how mankind can dream up such silly ideas.)

As God says in Ezekiel 18:4, "⁴Behold, all souls are mine; as the soul of the father, so also the soul of the son is mine: the soul that sinneth, it shall die."

How many times have you heard it preached in your "church" that you've got to give your soul to God? That teaching is false; you cannot give your soul to God because He already owns it and always has, and guess what, He can do with it whatever He chooses.

What will be your decision concerning this demise of your soul? Will you choose to follow Satan and man's imaginations and be blotted out of the book of life?

God has given us the gift of free will so that we can choose our own destiny. I want you to take an inventory of all the things that you have been taught. Get some paper and make two columns on it. On the left side, I want you to write down the things that you've been taught concerning God's Word all during your lifetime. Be honest with yourself and write those teachings and beliefs down. Now on the right side, write what God's true word says as you learn the truth when you go through this book. Then you can see for yourself that more than likely you have been misled by listening to false doctrines preached by false preachers. God wants you to get away from all that nonsense and listen to Him. He wants you to educate yourself to the point that, using common sense and your newfound knowledge, you can spot those windbags in five minutes. That red flag will go up in your mind, and you'll find yourself amazed that a so-called man of God would get behind that pulpit and fill people's minds with soul-devouring lies of deception.

God's ways are the only way to true salvation. There is no other way that exists. It's a personal thing between *you and God*. Why would you want to listen to these nutcases? Because it feels "so holy?" Truth is the only way to true salvation. (Don't listen to garbage.)

God's way is so easy and simple.

Do things God's way by accepting Him as your Savior. You do this by faith, *true* faith; but you are instructed by God that you cannot stop there. You must study to show yourself approved. Why study? Well, that is the only way for you to see if you have been taught truth, or have been taught lies instead. That's exactly the reason why you *must* study. Never believe anything unless you can verify it in God's Word.

Remember that the great controversy is between God's and Satan's teaching and the temptations Satan lures you into. (Believe me, he is winning for now. He's winning big time!) When Satan comes here in person, God says the whole world will follow him (except for those who do know truth). Look at the deception that abounds. Look at the lies. Look at our country's massive debts. Look at the *pride* in which these elected politicians strut around. Look at the massive waste of our so-called money. Look how the value of our money is fading. Look at all the religions of the world. Are any of these confusing to you? Are you being deceived?

You'll hear nothing deceiving from our Heavenly Father. He is my Father, He is your Father, and He is everyone's Father; He is everything. Let's follow God—and to hell with Satan!

Sorry there is *no other way* except by Him.

Get away from "man's traditions" of generational false teachings. Don't be deceived. Most people are deceived though. Most people wear that false cloak of deception and feel cozy with it on, and that's a sad thing to see.

Man's time is a fleeting thing. Better use it wisely! *Don't be sottish.* I love this word *sottish* as God uses it (it means stupid). He does teach straight on and to the point. If you get upset by His frankness, then please Him by getting your act together. Study and learn what God has to say concerning *all* things. Don't listen to "man's traditions." If you do, you're stupid! (Now I did not call you stupid. God did.) He calls us sottish if we choose Satan instead of our very Creator, God.

The Third Earth Age

At the end of Satan's five-month reign that God has allowed begins the third earth age, and this age will be a very busy time for *all* people who has ever lived since God first created mankind.

The Lord's Day (the Millennium) will finally begin and *only* truth will be taught to those who did not have the opportunity to hear its purity without being distracted by Satan and his evil spirits. At that time, Satan is safely locked away and guarded.

At the end of *the Lord's Day*, judgment begins. You have two choices. If you choose Satan, you go to Hell. If you choose our true Father, you'll be Heaven bound.

Satan will be turned loose for a short time to gather his many followers who still worship him and believe in his lies. They will follow Him straight to Hell to be blotted out and turned to ashes from within.

Can you believe that? After seeing God and hearing Him, many will *still* follow Satan. That is stunning but true!

After Judgment, those of us who are *tried and true* Christians will finally be rewarded with Heaven and have our Heavenly Father as our leader *forever and never ending*.

Too bad for you Satan followers, you will also receive *your* just reward. Hope you will enjoy it!

WHAT HAPPENS TO US WHEN WE DIE? (THE ROAD TO SALVATION)

Different religions have conflicting "theories" on this very vital subject. Denominations breed confusion, but there's no need to be confused. Let's deal in *facts*. Let's clear the air! Let's eliminate confusion.

God says in Mark 13:23, "²³But take ye heed: [you people listen to me] behold, I have foretold you all things."

(And indeed He has!) So the *facts* begin.

Facts 1 and 2

There is one earth but there are three earth ages (three spans of time). God created *all* of us in the *first* earth age. He created us then in our angelic spiritual bodies. The creation of *us* happened long, long ago—thousands, if not millions of years ago. (No *exact* number of years is Biblically recorded.) We still possess today our angelic bodies, our souls. Satan was also created at the same time as we were, and because of Satan's *pride*—thinking he could become God himself—a great rebellion occurred. (There is much more written in this book about this rebellion.) So God said to all of us, "I will make mankind, to look exactly like we look." So God placed our angelic bodies (our souls) inside our flesh bodies where they dwell today. When our flesh bodies die, our souls return to our Father in paradise. (It's just that simple!)

Fact 3

When God created mankind in the flesh, the *second* earth age began. This age, when compared to the span of time of the first age earth, is very, very short. It has a time span of only eight thousand to fourteen thousand years. (The generation that we are living in today *is the last generation*! The sands of time is quickly coming to an end. The last grain is about to fall. God has said it and therefore it is truth. God cannot lie.)

Do you believe in God?

Now going back to that first earth age, there arose a great controversy between our Heavenly Father and the idiot, named Satan. Satan had his followers (about four billion souls) and our Father had the rest (about eight billion). This is a rough but close estimate. The controversy continues to this day. Soon Satan will return to gather his followers, and guess what? Almost all people will follow him. It is written that the whole world's population, except for God's chosen elect, will follow him. (Look around us today, evil is ruling, evil is supreme!)

Fact 4

Our Heavenly Father was very disappointed concerning Satan's success, and it was a crushing hurt that so many had turned against Him in that first earth age. He had to make a decision. He could put Satan and his followers to death, or He could try something else. So He created the *second earth age* and created man in the flesh. He placed the soul (the angelic, spiritual body) into their flesh bodies to come through the womb and be born of the water (like all babies are born this very day). Our appearance, in the flesh, is as we looked in our angelic bodies. Exactly! We are carbon copies!

Fact 5

In Genesis 1:26–27, [26]God said "Let us make man in our image, after our likeness: and let them have dominion over the fish of the sea, and over the fowl of the air, and over the cattle, and over all the earth, and over every creeping thing that creepeth upon the earth. [27]So God created man in his *own* image, in the image of God created he him; male and female created he them."

Fact 6

God created man for one main purpose. He wants to see how mankind will handle Satan's temptations of false teachings coming from the lying lips of false preachers. These so-called preachers who teach lies in their so-called churches *are not* sent by God our Father, but instead by Satan *their* father. (Yes, there are *two* fathers; one real, the other one false.) Which one are you following? That's the big question.

Fact 7

If we choose the false Christ here in this second earth age, then we go to paradise with a mortal (liable to die) soul. Your soul is Hell bound at this point.

Fact 8

Our mortal souls must put on immortality (deathlessness) to achieve Heaven and become a partaker of all of God's creations and preparations awaiting all who have remained steadfast with Him. Words alone cannot describe the beauty that will abound. All evil will have been done away with.

Fact 9

At Judgment Day, all mortal souls (those who chose Satan and his lies) will be blotted out. They will no longer be around. They'll follow *their* father to utter extinction. Don't feel sorry for them because they had free will (like in the first earth age) to choose their own fate. So good riddance!

Fact 10

All flesh will die; sooner for some, later for others. Some die in accidents, some die defending their country, some are murdered, and some die by their own hand. The point being: We *all* will die—it's a sure thing.

Fact 11

At that moment of death of our flesh bodies, our souls (angelic or spiritual bodies) instantly leave and return to God.

As God says in Ecclesiaster 12:7: "⁷Then shall the dust return to the earth as it was: and the spirit shall return unto God who gave it" and in 1 Corinthians 15:44, it is written that "⁴⁴It is sown a natural body; it is raised a spiritual body. There is a natural body, and there is a spiritual body."

Now let's recap all that we've learned and have locked-in in our minds up to this point:

1. Our souls were created in the *first* earth age.
2. Then God created our flesh bodies and placed our spiritual bodies inside these in the *second* earth age.
3. All of us went down the highway of life until, at whatever age, we will die.
4. All our flesh bodies returns to the soil from whence it came.
5. All our angelic bodies returns to God from whence it came.

The *serious* results of life in these flesh bodies, in reality, begins at death. Depending on our life's choices, we get Heaven or we get Hell. God is *the* Judge, the *only* Judge. God is always fair. Every person gets their own individual reward. Some rewards are good! Some are bad!

This is the reason I have told you that *Christianity is a reality, not a religion.* People can follow many religions. They can be taught many things, but if these conflict with God's *true* word, and if they believe and follow the misinformation that turns out to be false, then they will find themselves with a *very big problem.* You *must* learn truth.

If all the things that you have been taught did *not* align with God's actual true teachings, then you've been had. You listened to lies and believed in nonsense.

You will also find out that the words *religion* and *denomination* mean absolutely nothing to God.

A religion cannot save you!

A denomination cannot save you!

No preacher or church leader can save you!

The saving of your soul from Hell can be accomplished *only* by a personal relationship between you and our Heavenly Father.

You need to talk to Him one-on-one, repent all of your sins, and follow His commandments as best you can during your lifetime.

Learn God's truth. Don't listen to nonsense!

All the so-called holy rituals that you were taught were actually dreamed up by man, not God. God calls them "man's traditions" and instructs us to steer clear of the *vain imaginations*. So do it.

(But in the end, you have no one to blame but yourself if you don't follow God's advice and demands.)

At the death of these flesh bodies, we find ourselves instantly at that juncture at the end of "life's highway."

One of God's trusted people will meet you at that juncture to point you either to the bad side or the good side.

(I look at this as a prejudgment of sorts.)

Both sides are called *Paradise* by our Heavenly Father, and we will *all* be there until the Great White Throne Judgment takes place at the very end of the Millennium.

Always remember these verses from Luke 16:19–31:

> [19]There was a certain rich man, which was clothed in purple and fine linen, and fared sumptuously every day: [20]And there was a certain beggar named Lazarus, which was laid at his gate, full of sores, [21]And desiring to be fed with the crumbs which fell from the rich man's table: moreover the dogs came and licked his sores. [22]And it came to pass, that the beggar died, and was carried by the angels into Abraham's bosom: the rich man also died, and was buried; [23]And in hell he lift up his eyes, being in torments, and seeth Abraham afar off, and Lazarus in his bosom. [24]And he cried and said, Father Abraham, have mercy on me, and send Lazarus, that he may dip

the tip of his finger in water, and cool my tongue; for I am tormented in this flame. [25]But Abraham said, Son, remember that thou in thy lifetime receivedst thy good things, and likewise Lazarus evil things: but now he is comforted, and thou art tormented. [26]And beside all this, between us and you there is a great gulf fixed: so that they which would pass from hence to you cannot; neither can they pass to us, that would come from thence. [27]Then he said, I pray thee therefore, father, that thou wouldest send him to my father's house: [28]For I have five brethren; that he may testify unto them, lest they also come into this place of torment. [29]Abraham saith unto him, They have Moses and the prophets; let them hear them. [30]And he said, Nay, father Abraham: but if one went unto them from the dead, they will repent. [31]And he said unto him, If they hear not Moses and the prophets, neither will they be persuaded, though one rose from the dead.

(This simply means that there will be no going back and forth from the bad side to the good side and vice versa.)

You must keep in mind this scripture from Ezekiel 18:3 where God says, "[4]Behold, all souls are mine; as the soul of the father, so also the soul of the son is mine: the soul that sinneth, it shall die."

(I suggest that you read the entire chapter of Ezekiel 18 for it will give you great insight concerning our father's expectations of us as we travel this highway of life.)

Since God "owns all souls," that gives Him the right to do whatever He wants to with these. He is the Judge, and nobody gets away with anything. He sees *all* and hears *all*.

(All you false teachers and atheists and extreme taxers of the people out there, you'd better listen up! Your "payday" is quickly approaching.)

They say a picture is worth a thousand words! So I've prepared a picture to show you exactly as things *are* and how things *will be* (see chapter 12).

The Millennium (the Lord's Day) lasts one thousand years in man's time, but it amounts to only one day in God's time.

It is a time of teaching God's truth only, but many, if not most, will adhere to the lies that they were taught while here in the flesh. If they do, it's *hello Hell?* How sad!

Since our Father and our Creator is totally fair, He knows a person must hear God's truth before he can totally make up his or her mind as to where he decides to end up (Heaven or Hell). (Do you choose Satan or do you want to *wake up* to reality and take God as your Savior?)

During the Millennium *teachings of truth*, Satan and his spirit are locked away so that he will have *no* negative influence whatsoever on anyone.

At the end of the Millennium, they will be released for a short while, and you can believe it, many will *still* follow him to Hell and be eradicated along with Satan, *their* father. (How ignorant can a person get!)

God says in Matthew 10:28, "28And fear not them which kill the body, but are not able to kill the soul: but rather fear him which is able to destroy both soul and body in hell."

So there you have it, the beginning and the end. These are all facts from God's Word, so you must count it as the *gospel truth*. Truth will save you, lies will erase you! Don't listen to lies.

Who will *you* choose?

SPEAKING IN TONGUES (IT'S GIBBERISH)

Speaking gibberish is to God mockery at its fullest.

If you are of a faith that practices this nonsense stuff, you need to stop it. You are bordering on blasphemy.

It is beyond me that any preacher would teach you this garbage, but people being people will believe anything, I suppose.

The word *tongues* simply means *languages*. There are many languages in this world, but there is no language named gibberish.

So if you speak gibberish, it is a language that absolutely no one can understand. How silly!

God does *not* speak nor even understand gibberish. The people that speak it don't understand one another either. You are making an absolute *fool* of yourselves! Don't be ignorant and don't claim that "the Holy Spirit" came over you and overwhelmed you and spoke through you or gave you those words of gibberish to spew uncontrollably from your mouth. It's a stupid thing to be doing that, and all *true* Christians know it. So quit it, repent, and move on. Your preacher is an uneducated idiot. God calls him *sottish*.

Now we *let God speak* about tongues and why the "cloven tongue" is so special. *(Keep in mind that tongues mean languages, not gibberish.)*

We read in Acts 2:1–15:

> [1]And when the day of Pentecost was fully come, they were all with one accord in one place. [2]And suddenly there came a sound from heaven as of a rushing mighty wind, and it filled all the house where they were sitting. [3]And there appeared unto them cloven tongues like as of fire, and it sat upon each of them. [4]And they were all filled with the Holy Spirit, and began to speak with other tongues, as the Spirit gave them utterance. [5]And there were dwelling at Jerusalem Jews, devout men, out of every nation under heaven. [6]Now when this was noised abroad, the multitude came together, and were confounded, because that every man heard them speak in his own language. [7]And they were all amazed and marvelled, saying one to another, Behold, are not all these which speak Galilaeans? [8]And how hear we every man in our own tongue, wherein we were born? [9]Parthians, and Medes, and Elamites, and the dwellers in Mesopotamia, and in Judaea, and Cappadocia, in Pontus, and Asia, [10]Phrygia, and Pamphylia, in Egypt, and in the parts of Libya about Cyrene, and strangers of Rome, Jews and proselytes, [11]Cretes and Arabians, we do hear them speak in our tongues the wonderful works of God. [12]And

they were all amazed, and were in doubt, saying one to another, What meaneth this? [13]Others mocking said, These men are full of new wine. [14]But Peter, standing up with the eleven, lifted up his voice, and said unto them, Ye men of Judaea, and all ye that dwell at Jerusalem, be this known unto you, and hearken to my words: [15]For these are not drunken, as ye suppose, seeing it is but the third hour of the day.

God created all the languages way back in the Old Testament in Genesis 11:1–9 as a punishment for building the Tower of Babel (Babel means confusion).

These Tower of Babel builders were trying to build their own stairway to Heaven, or better said, they were attempting to build another way to salvation; but the tower fell, just as confusion falls.

Confusion has no legs to stand on! Babel always falls.

So with all the new languages, no one could understand what the others were saying to one another, but as time passed man adapted and today we *can* understand.

We can understand *all* languages except *gibberish*!

It *is nonsense* to the *n*th degree.

7

THE PRAYING OF PRAYERS

Do you pray to our Heavenly Father from the depths of your heart, or do you pray from a written prayer? Do you pray with repetitive mumblings that you were told would be the "holy" way to pray? Do you pray only because it is the custom of your particular religion? Do you use hand signs or other body languages in your prayers? Do you do prayer because it is a ritual practiced through the generations and passed on down to you? Do you pray to angels? Or do you even get around to prayer?

It truly amazes me at the many ways "to pray" that mankind has dreamed up since the beginning of time as we know it. It's absolutely astounding, and sometimes it's downright silly.

I've seen and heard people pray in all those different methods, but as a young person I realized that praying to God is a very personal thing. *Nothing* is more personal than sincerely talking to our Creator one-on-one. He is supernatural, you know, and so very loving and understanding. He knows your needs, but He expects us to repent to Him of our sins thus wiping the slate clean so that we can truly pour our hearts out to Him. In return, God's blessings will flow back to us.

Our Father never sleeps. His door is open 24–7. He wants our *love* above all else. He desires that you know Him personally. To know Him is to love Him! *Tell* him that you love Him; He would love to hear from you.

God says in Hosea 6:6, "⁶For I desired mercy, and not sacrifice; and the knowledge of God more than burnt offerings."

Can you see the tenderness in the way God speaks to us with such a kind and gentle manner? He is so real. God wants you to give this verse some very deep thought. God's desires are within that verse—*love* and *knowledge.*

By having the knowledge of God's Word through studying, you cannot keep from seeing His sincere desires of wanting to hear the words like these coming directly from us saying: "I love you Father, and I need to talk to you about this problem that's bothering me." God is *real and actual.* He's not a spook! (He's not some force floating around out there.) He wants to hear from us and *prayer* is the only way to communicate with Him. He wants to give you blessings, true blessings. (By the way, in the Bible, the translators have written *Holy Ghost.* I would love for those two words to read *Holy Spirit*, which would actually be correct.)

It defies the imagination of all the wonderful things that our Father has done and is still doing for us every day.

And we all need to thank Him daily for the great and bountiful country that we enjoy here. Just think of the rich soils that produce even more food than we can eat. Think of the air we breathe. Think of our heritage.

Never pray to impress the listeners in the congregation in your church or at your dinner table. For that matter, how many people do you think attend church simply to be seen? Answer: A bunch of them! They have that "special pew." They like to sit (probably in the front row) so that everyone can see them. The wife will often be sporting the latest fashion for all to see and admire so as to be the envy of the day. (That's real Christian–like, isn't it?)

If the pastor asks them to lead the congregation in prayer, you'll most often hear the same memorized words time and time again (and sometimes I've even picked up a little "politics" mixed in their prayer. Oh, surely not!)

With all this being said, I'll simply urge you to sincerely pray and communicate with our Father on a daily basis and be sincere about it. You don't need to even pray out loud. He knows what you think at all times. God loves silent prayer.

Communication opens many doors. I personally like silent prayer because to me it seems much more personal and most of all it is private. It is no one's business about the many things I talk to my Father about. It's one-on-one, and I prefer that. I think He does too. You should pray daily so that you can experience that *personal touch* to you directly from Him. Do not put yourself in a position that when you die, and you meet God face-to-face He can say: "Who are you?"

Never ever confess your sins to another man as some churches teach and demand. (If you'll give that a little thought, you'll see how stupid that is.) Why would you ask *another man* to pray to God for *your* forgiveness? Only God can forgive, and you don't need any mortal man to be your "go-between." God does not like for a person to confess His sins to another person but only to Him. If you've been taught to do that, then you have been misled. (Lying preachers are doing Satan's work, not God's. God warns us throughout His word of this nonsense. *Common sense* has been thrown out window it seems.)

God is not a respecter of persons. This means that a garbage man is on the same playing field as those so-called holy men. How ignorant can mankind get? You need to get as far away from those crackpots (the ones who have indoctrinated you with such nonsense) as fast as you can. So *flush* all that malarkey out of your mind. Do it now. Don't wait another day.

One thing that I have always wondered about is this:

How can any so-called religion construct these massive buildings, many costing millions of dollars and some costing even in the hundreds of millions and even billions of dollars and justify doing so while children all over the earth are starving and dying daily due to malnourishment and disease? How can these so-called church leaders ever justify that "stuff" with our Heavenly Father? (Again we have *common sense* thrown out the window!)

God holds His little ones very, very close to His heart and it is our responsibility to take care of these children. God especially loves His orphans, and they all need that *special tenderness.*

It is not God's fault that they are in this dilemma, it is mankind's fault. When the so-called church leaders meet their maker, how are they going to answer Him? Are they going to say that they wanted to appear "holy" to the world through their "traditions?" Are they going to say that these expensive buildings were a necessity to get people in so that they can save souls? (Remember I told you earlier that God owns all souls, and no man can save a soul—any soul. Only God can.) Are they going to say that people needed this so that they could have a sacred place to "meditate and pray" to our Heavenly Father?

God will judge these so-called "spiritual men of God" with a rod of iron. He will even judge their so-called houses of worship (churches). It will not be pretty sight to watch God's wrath come down on them.

In Mark 13:1–2, God says: "¹And as he went out of the temple, one of his disciples saith unto him, Master, see what manner of stones and what buildings *are here*! ²And Jesus answering said unto him, Seest thou these great buildings? there shall not be left one stone upon another, that shall not be thrown down. And in Matthew 24:2, we read "²²And Jesus said unto them, See ye not all these things? verily [truly] I say unto you, There shall not be left here one stone upon another, that shall not be thrown down."

Why would God do such a thing? It is because He knows of the corruption that has gone on inside these buildings.

In these buildings, lies are being taught even to this day. God is going to cleanse this earth of sin and nonsense, and the buildings wherein these *things* are taught will exist no more (and I'll add, *good riddance!*).

Why would God cleanse something "so holy" such as mankind's "holy temples" that they have constructed? Why would He? Could it be because the lies of deception are being taught inside? Church socials with food are going on inside? You decide.

Well when we cleanse something, it always means that it's dirty. Why else would we wash it clean? We don't like dirty stuff, and neither does God. God can cleanse and instantly something becomes nothing. (Give this deep thought.) Payday is on its way! "Man's traditions" will instantly become nothing. (Sit back and watch!)

God knows all the *things* that are going on inside these so-called houses of worship and prayer, and He is not one bit happy about it! Didn't you see the word *things* in Matthew 24:2? Our Father says that He is going to *cleanse* these things by *destruction*. So it *shall* happen exactly as it is written. He said it and that's that!

We don't need a "temple" to go into because God Himself *is* our temple and don't ever forget it. One more thing people should realize is:

Christianity *is not*—I repeat—*is not* a religion.

It is a reality—I repeat—*it is* a reality.

This is a *fact* and it is *not* open for debate!

Amen.

HOPE
(WE ALL HAVE IT, OR DO WE?)

Have you ever thought about the word *hope* and how such an important and necessary role in life that this word plays.

Without hope, we have nothing! Nothing at all!

Allow me to expound on it.

I believe hope is the *most*, and I mean *most* important word that is used not only our language but *all* the languages around the world.

God uses this most important word throughout the Bible. God invented the word *hope*. (For that matter, God invented good words.)

But the word has a *special* significance. Hope coincides with *wish*.

Then there's the book of Job written some 2000 years before Christ where *hope* is used sixteen times.

The first *recorded* use of the word *hope* in the Bible was written in the book of Ruth some 1200 years before Christ with Naomi explaining to her daughters that "I should have said, I have *hope*, if I should have a husband also tonight and also bear sons."

The second recording is in Ezra 10:2 concerning Israel, around 500 Bc, making a six hundred-year span before the word was used again.

And in the Psalms, written 1000 Bc, where *hope* is used twenty-two times. But chapters one through forty-nine basically cover Genesis and the events covered there in that first books.

So what have we learned? Answer: *Hope* has been the backbone of mankind since the beginning of this, the second earth age, being the flesh age of mankind.

We must have *hope* or we cannot live a life with any degree of happiness. Our lives would be empty without it. (Think deeply about this subject.) To exist, we *must* have hope.

How would one ever want to live without hope? How *could* we possibly live without hope? We all should hope that we have done enough good works so that we are rewarded with a ticket to Heaven, not Hell.

With the absence of hope, we lose *all* purpose for life itself; so instead we keep it alive as it should be.

So what is hope? What does the word mean? Expectation! I think it means different things to different people.

For instance, *false* "hope" is when a person comes face-to-face with God on Judgment Day and realizes that he or she took the wrong turn in life and that he or she is being sentenced to Hell to be blotted out of existence when all along they were so sure that they had been taught truth. They realize at the last minute that they had learned lies and also *believed* those. So their "salvation" was truly nonexistent. Then all of a sudden, they had no hope!

So we've learned that there is *true hope*, there is *false hope*, and, lastly, there can be *no hope*.

Question: Where does *your hope* fit in?

WHY WORRY!
(A WASTE OF TIME)

In this unsettled times, people are *worrying* more than ever before! Why? Well because of modern technology where people receive up-to-date information of the bad stuff going on anywhere and everywhere on earth. This information is mostly always negative and even catastrophic at times. We hear and see things at a speed that we've never seen in the past. (It gets kind of scary!)

So what are we to do? Well *worry* seems to be the word of the day. Everybody worries.

What does God tell us concerning worry or worrying?

In Mark 12:22–26, 29–32, God says:

[22]And he said unto his disciples, Therefore I say unto you, Take no thought for your life, what ye shall eat; neither for the body, what ye shall put on. [24]Consider the ravens: for they neither sow nor reap; which neither have storehouse nor barn; and God feedeth them: how much more are ye better than the fowls? [25]And which of you with taking thought can add to his stature one cubit? [26]If ye then be not able to do that thing which is least, why take ye thought for the rest? [29]And seek not ye what ye shall eat, or what ye shall drink, neither be ye of doubtful mind. [30]For all these things do the nations of the world seek after: and your Father knoweth that ye have need of these things. [31]But rather seek ye the kingdom of God; and all these things shall be added unto you. [32]Fear not, little flock; for it is your Father's good pleasure to give you the kingdom.

In verse twenty-two, Christ is telling His disciples not to worry (take no thought) about their food and raiment because one never knows what today or tomorrow will bring. We can be here today but gone tomorrow. (How true it is.)

Now this isn't to say that we should forget the importance of savings for old age, but Christ is here talking about something that is way more important than food and raiment, and that is to have *faith and trust* in our Savior, our Creator.

It's an insurance policy of sorts with *the kingdom* being the reward for those who put their trust and faith in Him for *He does know* what tomorrow brings.

God knows what we need more than we do, and He promises that if we'll do our part, He'll do His.

God is telling us that *to worry* is akin to *doubting* His power of true blessings to all true Christians that will put their love, faith, and trust in Him first and foremost and never lose it. Stay true to God.

We all need to use common sense in our lives. God expects that of us, but when we reach a point of no return we in that time need to remember these eight verses. Our Father will never let us down.

As Christ stated in verse thirty-two, not only does it give Him pleasure but that it gives Him *good* pleasure to help us when we are in need.

God is in control. He always has been and always will be. God is our Alpha (beginning) and our Omega (end) and if you have Him on your side, things will always, and I mean always, fall right into place. This is so true!

God is ever so powerful, and He is our Father—the Father of all mankind. How could anyone deny Him or His outreaching loving arms to each and every one of us? Sadly many do.

It's a huge mistake to go through this life without any consideration of our very Creator, our only *true* Father, and deny His love toward us.

Don't be a doubting worrywart!

A person *cannot* have a true faith and trust in God and be a worrywart at the same time. (It doesn't fit!)

Always remember Gods unending power!

As He says in Isaiah 45:12, "12I have made the earth, and created man upon it: I, *even* my hands, have stretched out the heavens, and all their host have I commanded."

Amen.

THE FOUR HIDDEN DYNASTIES (SATAN'S SINFUL WORKS)

Satan can accomplish absolutely nothing without God allowing it. God allows Satan's influence and evil spirits to infiltrate the four central powers (dynasties) that operate in the world around us, which in turn affects everyone's daily lives. You need to be aware! Be alert and learn.

Naturally it has always been God's wish that these central powers, which are located in each and every country, would operate keeping God our Father in the forefront of all decisions that are made. Every decision made affect the population of which we His children are involved. His children are *us—all of us*. (In other words, God has always wanted *purity* to reign with our world leaders.) But sadly, it *doesn't*! Watch the world events as they unfold. They *are not* of God, but of Satan.

These four central "powers" (I'll call them this) are:

1. Our political system
2. Our religious system
3. Our educational system
4. Our economic system

God's wish of *purity* within the four dynasties has been met with deaf ears and blind eyes. His wish has *not* been granted.

So let's explore these systems to see exactly what is taking place within them. God is not a happy camper!

You must remember the first sentence of this chapter. God has *allowed* Satan's evilness to worm its way into each of these dynasties if the people allow and, yes, they *are* allowing it.

Why would God allow such a thing? Answer: To show *us* firsthand how tricky and vile and subtle Satan can be, and to show us how easy it is for Satan to have his way while laughing at us!

One of Satan's names is "the destroyer;" and his goal is to carry these dynasties by infiltrating the minds of the leaders of all countries to a point of no return. This is a test from God to us, and we have *failed* the test *big-time*. People, by a huge majority, have literally *forgotten God*. They've left God out of the equation of their lives.

Look around you. Can you see the mess we're in? Can you see and feel the emptiness and the feelings of *lost hope* that surround us? Can't you see Satan's evil spirit running rampant throughout the world? Of course you can!

These four dynasties are hidden in *plain sight*, and the workers of iniquity—Satan's ilk—are as busy as bees doing his work!

The Political System

We have elected left-wing screwballs to run this country. They are bringing in socialism, the sister of communism, into our daily lives. (Do you think this nonsense is the work of our Heavenly Father?) God loves His children and He absolutely will never willingly put burdens on any of us, but Satan's workers sure will.

People put burdens on themselves, so don't blame God.

God has told us over and over and over again how to prosper and how *to be of good cheer*, but it appears that the population prefers to be weighted down with evil. How stupid.

These politicians are operating with the minds of children. God warned us also of this: that a "sign" of this end of generation is that we'd put these Antichrist acting *nuts* over us to lead us—and we did.

God warned us to *never* borrow money from other countries because we would become slaves to them and their evil beliefs, but we gave no thought to His demand; and look at the mess that we have gotten ourselves in. Our debts can never be paid off, but we cannot blame God, we *can* only blame the idiotic screwballs who are in power.

Look at the lies that come out of the mouths of most of our politicians. More and more lies every day,. Are *lies* approved by God? Of course not! God *cannot* lie! It is written!

God told us to never elect a stranger as our leader. But we did. (Look at the price that we are paying for going against God's demand.) We *must* rid ourselves of *all* these knuckleheads and do it quickly! They are *not* of God. It's a fact!

Look at the waste and corruption that is in our political system. Look at the greed. Look at the evilness.

Now can you see that Satan's evil spirits are in all these?

Always remember: God's spirit is of *good* things. Satan's spirit is of *bad* things.

(Come on people, do we really want *bad* in our lives?)

Our Religious System

God hates religions and denominations. Why? Denominations mean division, with everyone believing something different. It's just that simple! If you love God, there is no need to be divided concerning His word. Denominations are easy pickings for Satan! He is *the* master of deception! (They come no better.)

Concerning *God's Word*, everything is *absolute*!

Denominations are strictly man's doing, not God's. God is a winner. Denominations are losers. (A *wise* thing for you to do is to give some very deep meditation to what I'm saying here, and you'll be able to see that God is *right* as always.) Satan is a loser. Don't join him.

God is good to us, but a day of reckoning is near. Being on the bad side of God on Judgment Day is a dangerous and unwise place to be. As for religions, it's a circus out there! People will believe anything no matter how radical the religion or what it believes in. We've got religions that love to kill Christians in the name of *their* god, we've got religions that believe in the rapture, religions that believe there is no God, religions that believe that Heaven or Hell is a "state of mind" and that neither is actually real. We've got religions that like music in their church and others who don't believe in music at their church. There are religions that worship idols and so on and so forth. (I'm sure you get the point.) Let me add that there are even Satan-worship religions!

Satan is also the author of confusion. Are people confused concerning religion? Yes, they are. Now more than ever!

People are *hoping* that they've chosen the right religion and this is a very sad fact. They *should* keep it simple—choose God. People do not need the fancy trappings of a building to make it to Heaven.

Religions are nonsense to our Heavenly Father. You can easily see that a religion *can* be the "sin of all sins."

People need to take inventory of their individual beliefs and come to the realizations that: True Christianity is a reality, *not* a religion, or better said, *Christianity is not a religion, it is a reality*. People as a whole go to the church of their choice but most often because mama and papa as well as grandparents all went to the same church. Their minds are filled with the doctrines and customs of "man's traditions" in their particular religions, and they become so staunch in believing in the rituals to a point that it becomes "fighting words" for anyone to criticize them. No religion can buy you a free pass to Heaven nor can a church leader. It is impossible.

God wants you to *think for yourself*. He abhors brainwashing, and I assure you, most people *are* brainwashed.

God has *foretold us all things*, so the questions remain, "Have you read? Do you know these things? Do you know *any* of God's promises to *you* personally?"

God made this statement in Isaiah 43:26, "²⁶Put me in remembrance: let us plead together: declare thou, that thou mayest be justified."

God is telling us here to remind *Him* of His personal promises to each and every one of us. It isn't that *He* doesn't remember, but He wants to see if *you've* done your homework. Do *you* know of His promises?

Trust me when I say to you that God demands that *we* have knowledge of His promises. You'll be unable to say: "Wait, let me run over here and get my preacher." No, no you are on your own face-to-face with our Heavenly Father. Are you prepared for this meeting? You'd better be! You had better get it right the first time around because there are *no* second chances!

You had better get yourselves prepared because this meeting *will* take place. (It's as sure as the sun rising in the east and setting in the west!)

God says in this verse that He wants to justify you, which simply means to make things *right* with you.

Now as a reward for doing your homework, here is just one of His promises as He says in Isaiah 43:25, 15 that "[25]I, *even* I, *am* he that blotteth out thy transgressions for mine own sake, and will not remember thy sins. [15]I *am* the LORD, your Holy One, the creator of Israel, your King"

Now, do you want your sins blotted out or would you rather have you yourself blotted out?

Study, to show yourself approved. This too is written.

Our Educational System

Our educational system is also infiltrated with Satan's evil spirits. Our children's minds are being brainwashed with evil nonsense, such as eliminating God from their school textbooks and other reading materials. (The children should be allowed to be *taught* and to be allowed to learn God's truth in the classroom on a daily basis. God would be pleased, and the little ones would love it. But the courts have made it taboo by passing laws to appease the "Satan lovers." How atheistic is that?)

Praying to our one and only Heavenly Father is a no-no, and therefore they are being taught to never mention His name nor to wear any types of clothing that even hints of anything that pertains to God or His Holy word. The courts have decided that using God's name is offensive! Wow! Why can't they see that they are slapping our very Creator right in the middle of His face? That's bad!

So let me ask you: Do you think that these children are going to grow up as good Christian citizens, or will they be atheists? Will they turn out to be agnostics? How do you think God feels about this "slap in the face?" Do you think that the people who put these laws into effect will get off scot-free when they have their personal one-on-one encounter with God? No they won't, I assure you! It is written.

Our children should have that daily class set aside to learn the most important subject in this world—*God's Word.*

If any parents resent God's teachings, then let them take their kids somewhere else or maybe homeschool them. And at home they can teach the little ones trashy nonsense. Let them teach their children that there is no God. But we should *not* cater to screwballs!

(What has happened to "our Christian nation?" Could it be Satan at work?)

Oh yes, take God out of everything. Go ahead, kick Him to the side. Yep, that's a smart thing to do!

Then when our children go off to college, they most likely will get hit with a nutty atheistic left-wing professor to help them finish off their personal "fine and expensive liberal education," and then they move on into society knowing absolutely nothing about the most important knowledge they *should* have, which concerns *true Christianity* and the fact there actually is a *true God* and Savior Jesus Christ.

Our Economic System

How are things going economically for you? Well let me promise you that things will be getting worse, not better! More burdens are in store for us, so be ready for them. We haven't seen anything yet. Stay tuned in, watch and listen.

When we allow Satan to enter and influence our world's systems, we can *never* have true peace in our lives because Satan is evil. (But God has already sentenced Satan to death.)

As God says, "¹⁸Thou hast defiled thy sanctuaries by the multitude of thine iniquities, by the iniquity of thy traffick; therefore will I bring forth a fire from the midst of thee, it shall devour thee, and I will bring thee to ashes upon the earth in the sight of all them that behold thee" (Ezekiel 28:18).

Haven't you noticed that our purchasing power has all but vanished? The ones that are involved with running our economy almost daily want more and more and more. I believe that many of them stay awake at night, trying to think of new ways to come up with more taxes. It's a fact. The more burdens that they can place on us, the happier they are. It's outright treasonous! (But it's our own fault. We, the people, put these nuts in office.)

Surely you don't think that God would handle business in such a haphazard manner, do you? God doesn't add burdens on His children, and He hates those who do. I assure you.

God warned us long ago that these things will come down on our head *if* we leave Him, our very Creator, out of our lives. (And we have for the most part.) Mankind has really messed things up! There is no turning back, it's much too late.

Yep, Satan is winning for now! Be patient though because Christ is also returning to set things straight with His *rod of iron* and His *cup of wrath*.

Amen.

8

THE GRAVE
(WILL WE RISE UP?)

When we die, we are buried. We are buried with our head toward the west and our feet toward the east as it is always mostly done.

This custom has gone on for many centuries and other than it being a simple custom, it serves no actual purpose. It is a false belief. It is a false custom.

People have always believed that when they rise up at the return of Christ, they'll instantly be facing the east where Christ will be located.

I can tell you with assurance that no graves will open and no one will rise up. When we are put in the ground, we stay there. We return to dust.

Most of us are old, wrinkled, worn out, and diseased. Why would we want these old bodies anyway? They are worthless.

What does God tells us about death and beyond?

In Ecclesiastes 9:5, 10, 12, God says:

> ⁵For the living know that they shall die: but the dead know not any thing, neither have they any more a reward; for

the memory of them is forgotten. [10]Whatsoever thy hand findeth to do, do *it* with thy might; for *there is* no work, nor device, nor knowledge, nor wisdom, in the grave, whither thou goest. [12]For man also knoweth not his time: as the fishes that are taken in an evil net, and as the birds that are caught in the snare; so *are* the sons of men snared in an evil time, when it falleth suddenly upon them.

And further in Ecclesiastes 12:6–7, "[6]Or ever the silver cord be loosed, or the golden bowl be broken, or the pitcher be broken at the fountain, or the wheel broken at the cistern. [7]Then shall the dust return to the earth as it was: and the spirit shall return unto God who gave it."

As you can see in verse six, the breaking of the "silver cord" or "golden bowl be broken" simply means *the very second we die.* Verse seven teaches us that these old bodies return to dust, and our soul (spirit) returns to our Father who gave it to us, or better said, we return back to God from whence we came. See? It is no mystery!

In Ecclesiastes 12:13–14, it is written: "[13]Let us hear the conclusion of the whole matter: Fear God, and keep his commandments: for this *is* the whole *duty* of man. [14]For God shall bring every work into judgment, with every secret thing, whether *it be* good, or whether *it be* evil."

In these verses thirteen and fourteen, God is telling us what our duty is while here in these flesh bodies, and that on Judgment Day, we will be judged by our deeds.

If we took care of business and protected and fed our souls according to God's demands then we will inherit the following: "[1]For we know that if our earthly house of *this* tabernacle were dissolved, we have a building of God, an house not made with hands, eternal in the heavens" (2 Corinthians 5:1).

With the outlandish cost of funerals in this day and time, why spend the money or go into debt over a customary type of funeral?

Cremation saves a considerable amount of money, and God would approve of it. It achieves the same purpose. We simply get to the dust stage much faster and much cheaper.

GOD'S LAW OF LIBERTY (DOING THINGS GOD'S WAY)

Everybody loves to live a life of freedom in these flesh bodies. That's a well-known fact. Many men and women have died in combat to protect the liberties that we have in this land of opportunity, the United States of America, and I know that God has blessed those soldiers in a very special way, and thank you Lord for that blessing.

The *law of liberty* that is directly from God is ever so important for people to learn.

Question: Can you say, for an absolute fact, that you are truly a Christian (a Christ-man)?

It's easy to *say* that you are a Christian, but have you gained your *spiritual* freedom, which is far more important for mankind to obtain than physical freedom? By misunderstanding the meaning of spiritual freedom you may be putting on that proverbial fast-track-to-Hell. I realize that sounds harsh, but so be it.

Our Father has the perfect *law of liberty*, and it's written in the book of James so that we can, by our following these guidelines, become an acceptable man or woman who can be deemed as a true *child of God*.

God's *law of liberty* (if followed as best you can) will put you on that fast track to Heaven. This information can save our souls so that we can spend eternity with our Loving Father. (Wow, what a payday!)

In James 1:2–8, 16, God says through James (I'll explain as we go along),

²My brethren, count it all joy when ye fall into divers temptations; [With the *wisdom* that comes from God Himself, and passed on to us, (if we seek it) we can easily overcome absolutely *all* of life's trials and tribulations, in a breeze. "Divers" means different. *True* believers are in a minority, therefore different!] ³Knowing *this*, that the trying of your faith worketh patience. [You become mature by doing all things God's way because God Himself is suffering for long, meaning *very* patient.] ⁴But let patience have *her* perfect work, that ye may be perfect and entire, wanting nothing. [The word *perfect* means mature. Patience breeds complete maturity in all things.] ⁵If any of you lack wisdom, let him ask of God, that giveth to all *men* liberally, and upbraideth not; and it shall be given him. [All wisdom comes from God. God is wisdom. Sincerely ask for His wisdom and He'll joyfully *share* the blessing of wisdom with each and every individual, but the key is to simply *ask* and be sincere. Sincerity is the *key*.] ⁶But let him ask in faith, nothing wavering. For he that wavereth is like a wave of the sea driven with the wind and tossed. [God is telling us, "Do not be a doubter" to any of His true teachings. Don't be like a "reed in the wind." But by allowing and accepting God's beautiful wisdom, you'll become solid in the foundation of Christ. So be stable.] ⁷For let not that man think that he shall receive any thing of the Lord. [There will be no doubters in God's kingdom. This verse says a lot. You need to think deeply and take a complete inventory of the thoughts and beliefs buried inside your mind. Do you doubt *any* of God's Word? Have you been deceived by a false doctrine that is running rampant? If a person doubts any one bit of God's Word, then he is *not* a true believer.] ⁸A double-minded man *is* unstable in all his ways. [A person's mind needs to be focused on God's Word, and *only* God's Word. If you will truly study God's truths and absorb those truths in your mind, you will become stable. An unstable person in God's Word will *never* see Heaven. Do you know why? Because

people are weak. Flesh is weak. Flesh is lazy. Flesh likes to take the easy road to Heaven by putting on their "Sunday best," going to their church of choice to sit there listening to a bunch of hot air and *believing* any and everything that they are taught without checking it out in God's letter to us. Why won't people seek out *truth* on their own? By learning the knowledge of God's Word, it will give you the ability see for yourself whether you are being lied to by false and misleading doctrines and lying preachers. Verses seven and eight are God's dire warnings to us all, and they deserve profound meditation on our part.] [16]Do not err (be deceived,) my beloved brethren. [I personally have witnessed false teachings and false doctrines in *every* so-called religion. Now stay with me and listen to God's likes and dislikes concerning these practices.]

Does your church practice an Easter celebration? Don't you realize that these so-called Christian services are akin to throwing dung in the face of our Lord and Savior Jesus Christ? If you preachers would take time to learn the truth, you'd quickly put an end to this nonsense. It's an Easter disservice, not an Easter service. I'll explain.

Boiling and hiding these Easter eggs is a false teaching, and the churches, in their divine ignorance, has let this *heathen worship* (a work of the Antichrist) through the doors of their so-called religions, and God hates it!

Easter eggs, these "eggs of fertility" is actually a celebration of the sex goddess, Ishtar. This "celebration of spring" began long ago with orgies of quick like a bunny out in the woods. (Use your imagination.) It's a teaching of pure filth and is being passed on from generation to generation of all people by the pastors of all these places of worship. (Now, aren't they brilliant?) Why won't they do their homework? It's simple research.

The word *Easter* is used only one time—in the book of Acts— and the word was placed there by a false scribe, a Kenite. Kenites are Satan's offspring. (I'll bet you didn't know that.) These Kenites are among God's greatest enemies and have been since the birth of Cain, Satan's son, born to Eve in the Garden of Eden. (The Kenites will be discussed in another chapter. Don't miss it.)

This Easter nonsense needs to stop and be done away with *right now*. How can you face God, knowing you have all your life practiced this pagan holiday? (And of all places your churches!)

I'll promise you that this practice did not come from God or anywhere in God's Word. It doesn't exist. Mankind invented this stuff, and it is shameful!

Passover is the *true* celebration that *should* be observed. (A *true* Christian knows this.) *Passover* is the highest *Holy Day* of Christianity. The date of Passover falls *exactly* on the fifteenth day following the spring equinox and has *absolutely nothing* to do with Easter eggs and bunny rabbits. Our children's minds are being filled with "man's traditions" of filthy lies by allowing the teaching of such nonsense. God hates this with a deeply burning passion. (It's not a good thing to upset our Father!)

If you've got a Bible that teaches such lies, you'd better throw it in the trash because it does not represent God's teachings of truth. If it's not *of God*, then it becomes *of Satan*. Which teaching are you celebrating? Well you are doing Satan's works of deception, and through ignorance, you have brought it into your so-called church. So, are you a church or are you a playing church? (Give this profound consideration. God gave us a brain, so let's use it!)

The Antichrist has a negative influence in and on many practices in the churches of today, and he accomplishes this through the pulpits. False teachings are running rampant, and the pastors are simply passing on, from generation to generation, the traditions of man instead of God's actual truths that takes away the real significance of this very special and most sacred and highest holy day of the year! (Throughout the Bible, God warns us to *not*—absolutely *not*—allow, I repeat, not allow "man's traditions" to be taught in a house that you call a church. You are teaching Satan's stuff instead of God's holy truth. (If you are guilty of this false and misleading stuff, you've got a big problem.)

You are truly blessed if you attend a church that teaches you God's Word, and God's Word only, and teaches it line by line, precept by precept, and chapter by chapter. (It is nearly impossible to fully understand the Bible if you skip a verse here and a verse there. You need to begin from page one and continue on to the very end and to be taught by a *true* scholar, and that scholar is God Himself! Then a person is able to grasp the *full* truths that God wants us to know. Otherwise you will have learned little or maybe nothing at all. I'm talking serious business here—and when you meet God face-to-face, ignorance of His word is *no* defense.)

A pastor will be held responsible for his teachings (judgment begins at the pulpit). It is a dangerous *and* an immoral act for preachers to deliver false and misleading information because they are messing around with the ultimate destiny of that person's very *soul*. If a pastor cannot teach truth by omitting the traditions of man, he should immediately seek another type of employment. (I'm not against a truth-teaching pastor, but I'm deeply against lying preachers who preach deception. Just because grandpa said it, doesn't make it true.)

I *love* what God loves, and I *hate* what God hates. Deception is in no way written in God's law of liberty. Truth is what sets us free, but lies keep us spiritually bound. Do not bind your mind with deception! Don't be stupid.

Most church members take their pastor's teachings as fact because they have *faith* in his every word. If his teachings are deceptive, how can that member further God's *work* by passing on lies? They can't! The *guilty* pastors are bringing down a superburden upon themselves when God is passing out judgment. I wouldn't want to be in their shoes (they're not going to like it either because God is a *consuming fire*!).

If people have faith in *truth* (and truth only) then they *can* further God's works in a positive and productive manner.

Therefore they are truly following God's *law of liberty* and are *free*. Truth sets you free *but* lies bind you forever! Believing false teachings will bind you hand-in-hand with Satan himself, and that's a bad, bad thing.

Faith and works go together as God intended.

As God says in James 2:14–16:

> [14]What *doth it* profit, my brethren, though a man say he hath faith, and have not works? can faith save him? [Answer: no] [15]If a brother or sister be naked, and destitute of daily food, [think of this as a person being "destitute" to hear Gods' Holy truth instead of the "traditions of man." which is nothing more than "hot air." He's tired of hearing lies and He wants "truth," because He has come to the realization that God *is* the "bread of life," for all. And how true it is!] [16]And one of you say unto them, Depart in peace, be *ye* warmed and filled; notwithstanding ye give them not those things which are needful to the body [I'll add and soul]; what *doth it* profit? [Answer: nothing]

Spiritually speaking, how can you (preacher) help this needful person if everything you feed them are the traditions of men that you have taught them, and they in turn believe in these traditions, instead of the *meat* of God's Word? How can you live with yourself if you haven't *fed* them *truth*? Answer: God has the answer for you, and I don't think that you are going to like it one bit! Why don't you ask Him yourself?

Earlier in this writing, I quoted a scripture to you from God's Word that in these end times, people will not be starving for bread, but for hearing God's Word. So have faith in *truth* so that your *works* will be deemed pure. Don't allow yourself to be fed garbage. (Why? Because garbage in, garbage out!) Don't be like these undereducated lying wannabe preachers! They'll lie to you; God won't!

We must all, as *true* Christians, make hay while the sun shines. Life is short and fleeting, and a person's *works* is all that he or she can take with them when we die. Nothing else!

Always adhere to this following verse: "14Whereas ye know not what *shall be* on the morrow. For what *is* your life? It is even a vapour, that appeareth for a little time, and then vanisheth away" (James 4:14).

Two of my favorite verses that fit real well with God's *law of liberty* are written in the first letter of Peter, and they concern excellent definitions of both faith and works during this second earth age that we are going through in these flesh bodies.

Concerning faith, in 1 Peter 1:8–9, 17 God says (through Peter):

> 8Whom having not seen, ye love; in whom, though now ye see *him* not, yet believing, ye rejoice with joy unspeakable and full of glory: *9Receiving the end of your faith, even the salvation of your souls.* 17And if ye call on the Father, who without respect of persons judgeth according to every man's work, pass the time of your sojourning *here* in fear: [Fear used here *means reverence.*]

Here you can easily see the importance of *faith and works.* They fit together like a glove. A person cannot truly have *faith* in his heart without being eager to do God's will (work).

Work can be many things. It can be tending to the sick, the weak, or paying a smiling visit to the elderly in nursing homes that many times are "hidden away" by their very own children who couldn't care less about them. All positive works will be highly rewarded by our Father on the *true payday* that is soon to come.

However, whatever work you choose to do, you must always protect your credibility. It is oh so very important that you don't make a mockery of God or yourself. Have humility. I'll leave the subject of law and liberty with these two verses from 1 Peter 1:24–25 where God says, "24For all flesh *is* as grass, and all the glory of man as the flower of grass. The grass withereth, and the flower thereof falleth away: [25]But the word of the Lord endureth for ever. And this is the word which by the gospel is preached unto you."

(How wonderful and complete is God's written Word.)

Allow me to add these personal thoughts of truths:

> I hate misleading ignorant preachers because God does!
> I hate phony churches because God does!
> I hate ignorance because God does!
> I hate gossipers and backbiters because God does!
> I hate "man's traditions" because God does!
> I hate denominations because God does!
> I hate religions because God does!
> I hate corruption because God does!
> I hate atheists because God does!
> I hate impurity because God does!
> I hate idol-worshipers because God does!
> I hate thieves because God does!
> I hate Satan and *all* that he stands for because God does!
> I hate socialism because God does!
> I hate communism because God does!
> I hate pride because God does!
> I hate crooked politicians and judges because God does!
> I hate crooked cops because God does!
> I hate agnostics because God does!
> I hate warmongers because God does!
> I hate people who lie because God does!
> I hate people who break promises because God does!
> I hate murderers because God does!
> I hate child molesters because God does!

I could go on and on and on, but I want to make this statement: All of these *hates* can be eliminated if people would simply come to repentance and do a complete about-face in their thinking and their evilness, and *all*—and I mean *all*—things would be in complete harmony.

Christ wants harmony and, someday soon, He'll have it! (He'll have it one way or the other, and we will all witness it.)

Liberty *is* freedom, and *truth* sets us free!

Let me add this: I realize I come across very harsh while trying to teach you the dire need for people to learn God's true teaching, but I'm simply trying to wake you up to reality.

God does *not* like sugarcoated words. He wants His Word to be taught straight on. He wants preachers to teach His Word *exactly* as it is written. God is *firm* and *to the point*, and He detests beating around the bush utilizing political correctness. He loathes it!

I'm no preacher, pastor, or reverend. I'm simply a *true* Christian layman attempting to pass on truth to *you* and by doing so, I lay out the snares and pitfalls that Satan is using so that you'll be made aware of them all.

Satan knows that God has already given him the death sentence, and he wants to take down as many as he can with him, and I feel a need to educate you and warn you of Satan's coming that is about to take place.

God wants a *true Christian* to sound that warning! I hope that you are listening because I *am* sounding that *warning* to all of you, my brothers and sisters. I do this out of love for you! (I want to see you in Heaven.)

SATAN'S COMING

This is an introduction to the *king of deception*; his name is Satan. Satan is God's number one enemy and has been since soon after his creation in the first earth age.

Deception is, by far, the major theme of God's holy Word. Being deceived will cost many people to lose their souls, and as you'll learn, losing your soul is absolutely the very last thing left for you to lose. The following shows you how God assures you the way to *save* it.

No one with any sense of survival would ever want to lose the very last thing they have; but only God can save your soul. We all have free will, so choose God, not Satan.

Listen up! It is very simple; *if* you'll be open-minded enough to let God's Words of truth in your brain to consider and accept.

The key to destroy deception, which is truly Satan's most lethal weapon, is to trust and have faith in the words of pure truth from our Creator, our Heavenly Father, the Father of us all. He is our *actual* true Father. He is *the* Father of every race, creed, and color, and *He loves* His creation. God is not a respecter of persons, meaning that He loves all of us, and He loves us *all* equally the same. (We should throw racism out of the window. There is no room for racists. God does *not* approve of racism.)

So with this intro, we'll move forward. Read on remembering that *most* people *are* deceived, and only *a few* in the big picture *are not*.

How in this world can so many be deceived? Well here, according to God (our Father) is your answer: "⁸This people draweth nigh unto me with their mouth, and honoureth me with their lips; but their heart is far from me. ⁹But in vain they do worship me, teaching for doctrines the commandments of men" (Matthew 15:8–9).

God is *very* upset with lying fake preachers. They are *not* teaching God's Word! They are not teaching God's truth! They make up stories from la-la land simply to coincide with their "message of the day." It is pure and simple blasphemy, God says (and I say)—and I will assure you—that their just reward will be the death of *their* individual souls. (And they call themselves preachers of God's Word?) Get yourselves away from these lying deceivers who are causing havoc among the people. Don't lose your soul! (We, true Christians, realize that we're nobody in the big scope of things, but our hearts ache along with our Father, and we do sincerely hope that people will wake up to reality.)

Maybe they *will*. Maybe they *won't*.

The *wonts* are the losers. The *wills* always win!

The creator of the greatest deception of all times will be making his big-time appearance in this generation, the generation of the fig tree. God warns us about his coming all throughout His Holy word. It is not a secret. Satan and his seven thousand supernatural fallen angels will appear here on earth exactly five months before Christ's appearance.

He is a *supernatural* being who looks like you and me. He has many names, but we commonly call him Satan. Let's learn about him and his many names and how he came to be.

In Ezekiel 28:12–19, God says:

> ¹²Son of man, take up a lamentation [a sad song] upon the king of Tyrus [one of his names] and say unto him, Thus saith the Lord GOD; Thou sealest up the sum, full of wisdom, and perfect in beauty [Satan is a superterrestrial entity. God created him this way and gave him great powers. In the beginning, Satan was even elevated to the position of protector of the mercy seat, and God was proud of His creation]. ¹³Thou hast been in Eden the garden of God; every precious stone *was* thy covering, the sardius, topaz, and the diamond, the beryl, the onyx, and the jasper, the sapphire, the emerald, and the carbuncle, and gold: the workmanship of thy tabrets and of thy pipes was prepared in thee in the day that thou wast created [Notice that he was *created*, not *born* of woman]. ¹⁴Thou *art* the anointed cherub that covereth [guards]; and I have set thee <u>so</u>: thou wast upon the holy mountain of God; thou hast walked up and down in the midst of the stones of fire ["I was so proud of you Satan," God is saying to him]. ¹⁵Thou *wast* perfect in thy ways from the day that thou wast created, till iniquity was found in thee [Here comes God's fury by giving Satan the death penalty. Satan is the *only* one, *by*

name, who has been sentenced and judged to death even to *this* time. Can you see the opportunity we have, at this time, to get our business straight with God?]. [16]By the multitude of thy merchandise they have filled the midst of thee with violence [no morals] and thou hast sinned: therefore I will cast thee as profane out of the mountain of God: and I will destroy thee, O covering cherub, from the midst of the stones of fire. [17]Thine heart was lifted up because of thy beauty, thou hast corrupted thy wisdom by reason of thy brightness: I will cast thee to the ground, I will lay thee before kings, that they may behold thee [God is telling Satan: "Your pride got the best of you, and you really *do* think that you are smarter than me, your very Creator, and so that makes *you* my worst adversary. So, I'm going to let everyone *witness* your destruction (at the end of the Millennium). In the meantime, go ahead and spread your evil spirit far and wide, and see how many you can convince to follow you."]. [18]Thou hast defiled thy sanctuaries [with lies] by the multitude of thine iniquities, by the iniquity of thy traffick; therefore will I bring forth a fire from the midst of thee, it shall devour thee [by turning you to ashes from within] and I will bring thee to ashes upon the earth in the sight of all them that behold thee. [19]All they that know thee among the people shall be astonished at thee: thou shalt be a terror, and never *shalt* thou *be* any more. [Satan will finally meet his end, and we'll all see it with our very own eyes. I, for one, can hardly wait to see this come to pass. Satan's evil spirit is the "root" of negative influence on the people of this world. He makes positive things void. People seem not to realize the effect that Satan has in their everyday lives by his utilizing the vast powers that God gave him in the beginning.]

God is so good to us by letting us know the dangers that are upon us at all times, and He expects us to stay on full alert so as not to be taken in by Satan.

Most people are unaware of God's prophecies concerning Satan and his evil spirits that have slipped into almost everything that affects our day-to-day lives. Deception is the *root* of it all.

God wanted a *utopia* for us here on this beautiful and bountiful earth, but because of Satan's evil spirits it has turned into a living Hell, and it is getting worse every day. Why? Because people have not been taught *truth*, so they became easy prey to Satan. They follow his evil spirits while, in most cases, they don't realize it. Why? Answer: Because of ignorance of God's Word.

It seems that the pastors of today sugarcoat their messages to their congregations with those feel-good words to pump them up so that they can make it through another week and return again the next week to hear yet even more hot air. Pastors are not sounding the *warning of Satan's coming*. Their real job is to warn the people (us) of Satan's coming, but *they* don't seem to be aware of it.

Most pastors don't even *know* about Satan's coming!

Satan's return to this earth will happen exactly as God has told us. It is written!

Let's learn about it always remembering that we have two Gods to deal with in our lives. There is God (with a capital *G*) and there is a god (in a lower case *g*).

We *winners* serve *our* God. The *losers* serve *their* god. Do you want to be on the winning team, or do you prefer being a part of the losing team? Because God has given us free will, we have the ability to make that decision. It appears that most people have chosen the losing side. How sad! How ignorant!

Fact: Satan is coming.

When?

God says in 2 Thessalonians 2:3–4

> ³Let no man deceive you by any means: for that day [Satan's actual return day] shall not come, except there come a falling away first, [A falling away or denying truth from God Himself, and that falling away is happening by the

droves right now and that man of sin be revealed, the son of perdition. We are now near the end of the fifth trump. Satan will be here at the sixth trump.] ⁴Who opposeth and exalteth himself above all that is called God, or that is worshipped; so that he as God sitteth in the temple of God, shewing himself that he is God.

In the sixth trump, we are all still in our flesh bodies, so we who are in the know will recognize that it is Satan pretending to be the real God. He won't fool us one bit! Why? Because we've been properly educated in God's truth. We know that *our* Savior comes *after* Satan. Our Lord comes at the seventh trump.

The prophecy concerning Satan's coming is the *number one fact* that you have got to get burned into your mind so that you will *not* be deceived by *his* message. Always remember that we are in these flesh bodies when Satan appears, but at Christ's return we are instantly changed into our angelic bodies in the blink of an eye.

It is a shame that the pastors around the country aren't teaching this every time the church doors are swung open so that all peoples will know of the warnings and signs God has taught us, in His Word, about Satan's appearance, which is quickly approaching. This is the generation in which all prophecies shall come to pass. Most of us will actually witness these events.

Have you been taught that the generation of the fig tree is the very last generation in these flesh bodies? Hasn't your preacher taught you all about it?

Our Father has warned us over and over and over again about the signs and wonders that Satan will bring with him. This will be a time of testing for all peoples to see who's done their homework.

It is so sad to say, but most (nearly all) are *not* prepared for Satan's return at the sixth trump, and here is how I *know* that people are not prepared.

Our Father ordered Michael, God's archangel, to lock up Satan and the seven thousand of his fallen angels-followers "until further notice." However, Satan's evil *spirit* is allowed to roam this earth even today.

Satan's evil spirit alone has a huge impact on all current events, as we see in our news programs presented to us daily on TV, and everyone needs to pay attention to these unfolding news tidbits, for many of them are prophecies that are coming true in these end times.

Very soon, Satan and all his fallen angels will be cast out in person onto this earth, and the people will have to deal with him. We *must* be prepared.

God says in Revelation 12:7–9,

> [7]And there was war in heaven: Michael and his angels fought against the dragon [one of Satan's names]; and the dragon fought and his angels [the seven thousand], [8]And prevailed not [they lost]; neither was their place found any more in heaven [Why? God threw them out. They are sentenced to death]. [9]And the great dragon was cast out, that old serpent, called the Devil, and Satan, which deceiveth the whole world: he was cast out into the earth, and his angels were cast out with him. [Here the sixth trump has come to pass. Did you notice the many names that Satan goes by?]

Did you notice that Satan will deceive the *whole earth*?

Now you've already been shown that he has "full beauty" about him. He is not only a supernatural and a good-looking entity; he is so subtle that convincing mere mortal man that he is "Christ Himself" is a very easy task for him. (It's like taking candy from a baby!) Since people are so used to seeing Satan portrayed in long red undies and a wicked-looking pitchfork, people will be immediately deceived in thinking he's Christ.

People are deceived because they *have not been* taught that Satan comes first, claiming to be Jesus Himself, and naturally, through ignorance, people will instantly believe in him, the

Antichrist. They will find themselves deceived by him, the master of deceivers (what a shame).

(This is an alarm for people to wake up!)

This end-time deception is old news to us, the few who have been properly taught; but the real fault of people falling into Satan's net of deception *are the so-called pastors*, teachers, preachers, reverends (or by whatever name they wish to call themselves) who have slipped into the pulpits of our country, teaching very little concerning our Father's word but instead rather blow hot air and nonsense.

God says: "⁶From which some [wannabe preachers] having swerved have turned aside unto vain jangling; [all talk, empty teaching] ⁷Desiring to be teachers of the law; understanding neither what they say, nor whereof they affirm". (1 Timothy 1:6–7)

(They do not know where to back up their message in God's Word. Why? Because it probably *isn't* in God's Word; it is just *hot air* and whistling Dixie!)

There is a great hunger out there among the peoples of the earth. They are yearning to hear the *clear voice of truth*. The nonsense that people are being fed by preachers who have no understanding themselves is a shame and a disgrace.

A preacher's job is to warn the people of *all* prophecies that God set forth through *His* prophets. Many prophecies have come to pass, but the number one and the most urgent for people to understand *is* going to happen very, very soon. Satan's arrival is very soon. You can count on it. Some of us who are alive today will witness Satan's coming.

It is of the *utmost urgency* that people be taught that this is the fifth trump that we are living in right now, and it will soon end. It's a *fact*, not *fiction*. (This fifth trump is a time set aside for teaching. I'm doing my best to warn you to be alert and to be *in the know*.)

The fate of your very soul is in the *red zone* (meaning beware). Your brain needs to be nourished with *truth* so that you can be of a positive use in God's kingdom. It is our job to please our Father, and knowing truth will make His day.

The *great controversy* since the beginning of time (between God and Satan) is finally about to come to an end. The SOS is being sounded, and people need to be educated to a point that they know their feet are standing on solid footing!

Or better yet, people need to *know* that they are planted on *solid rock*, which *is* Christ. Satan's "rock" is *not* a solid rock. It is a very, very shaky rock because it stands for *nothingness* and will come to nothing. God assures us that Satan has been sentenced to death already. God gave him the *death sentence of all death sentences*, and praise God for it.

I want to say to you preachers and pastors out there: you should teach your flock that Satan returns at the sixth trump *claiming to be God*, and that God Himself returns at the seventh trump. This warning of Satan's return should be the main theme of *all* your sermons from now on! It is simply that urgent.

If you find that you don't have the knowledge to teach about this event of Satan's coming, then educate yourself to a point that you can teach it truthfully, or find yourself another line of work. Judgment begins at the pulpit, so beware—you have been warned.

Maybe you'd make a good janitor there at your so-called church, and since God warns all preachers that judgment begins at the pulpit, you won't be guilty any longer of blowing all that hot air of nonsense (and *that* would be a good thing!).

Our Heavenly Father has given Satan and his evil spirit many powers. You can see how these powers are affecting our everyday lives right now. Watch and listen.

In Revelation, Satan's four horns are mentioned and it is important for everyone to know the symbology of these four horns (*the four hidden dynasties*). Horns mean *power*, and, as we speak, Satan is entrenched in the use of these powers.

The four are *finance*, *education*, *politics*, and *religion*. (Let's do a quick overview of them.)

1. *Finance.* Excessive *usury* is a bad thing. Debt is a bad thing. God told us as a country to *borrow no money,* and He meant it.

Do our so-called leaders ever look at the *financial mess* the United States of America is in? (Do they really care?)

Do you think that these so-called whiz kids of finance have any financial sense? Of course they don't! Any idiot would know that we should never spend more than we take in. What has happened to the word *surplus*?

We, as a country, cannot control our spending. Our pocketbook is empty and has been for years. Many books could be written on finances as it pertains to this country, but we'll leave that to the "whiz kids!" (Since they are so brilliant!)

2. *Politics.* Surely no corruption exists here, does it? God told us long ago that our elected officials would act and handle business as children. It's so simple to see these "children playing" each and every day. They bicker back and forth as children. They have the minds of children. (Just as God told us it *would* be.)

They come up with fairy-tale dreams as children do. They have become way too expensive for our country to afford because, as children, they think they are playing with monopoly money instead of real money. They fly all over the world trying to take care of everybody's business when they can't even take care of our *own* business! Corruption abounds, and Satan's spirit is in the middle of it all. Our money says, "In God We Trust" (yeah, sure!). But maybe it should say, "Can God trust us?" (answer: no).

3. *Education.* Satan's work really shows here. The "brains" behind our educational systems are hard at work getting the word *God* out of everything we see and cherish. *God* has become a "bad word," and children should not say that "bad" word ever. It's not nice! All of these gutless wonders that are involved in the

mockery of our one and only Heavenly Father will have a special payday soon.

4. *Religion*. This is Satan's favorite playground, and he is doing an excellent job influencing our churches of today. He seems to have control over most of the preachers also. (This has already been discussed.)

So you can see that Satan's powers are working quite well. He is excellent at his job. He knows that most of the minds in this world are as shaky as a bowl of Jell-O. His job is "a piece a cake."

It's a very, very sad state of affairs! But not to worry; God will personally set things *straight* very, very soon.

The way people are ignoring God's Word is a very sad fact. God tells us *everything* in His word, but people ignore both Him *and* His word.

God is disappointed. It is such a disappointment that people are abusing Him by their evil deeds. It seems that most people are embarrassed to even *mention* His name in public or to even acknowledge His existence. (My heart hurts with Him.)

God has reached His limit concerning His patience with us. He has given so much to us, but we've failed to give anything back to Him though the only thing that He has asked for is our *love*.

God says: "⁶For I desired mercy, and not sacrifice; and the knowledge of God more than burnt offerings" (Hosea 6:6).

The reason we know that most people don't love God is in the things they say and do. The things they stand for has *evil* written all over it. It seems it's a replay of Christ's Crucifixion..

It is so sad about how our Creator is being treated, and *you* should feel sad about it too!

People need to repent. Now!

GOD FIGHTS THE TWO FINAL WARS

I'll set the stage by highlighting the people and events that are leading up to the final two battles: Hamon-Gog and Armageddon.

I have watched some preachers strike fear in the hearts of many people, and many even preach that the two battles lead to a nuclear obliteration of all mankind. Preachers should be ashamed for teaching such nonsense.

Let's learn the truth from God Himself. I often refer to God's scripture that says, "I have foretold you all things," and indeed He has.

In Deuteronomy 20:3–4, God says, "³And shall say unto them, Hear, O Israel, ye approach this day unto battle against your enemies: let not your hearts faint, fear not, and do not tremble, neither be ye terrified because of them; ⁴For the LORD your God *is* he that goeth with you, to fight for you against your enemies, to save you."

(God Himself is going to fight these last two battles alone. He needs no help. He will fight these battles to drive into the minds of *all* unbelievers and scoffers and mockers that *there is a God.* And to show that it is impossible to fight against God and win.)

If God is with us, who can be against us?

As in any war, there are opposing sides: the good, being the offspring of Jacob and later to be renamed Israel (this is us), and the bad, being Esau, Jacob's brother. Esau represents Russia for today and Jacob represents us America. So we have the two adversaries, Russia versus America.

In Malachi 1:2–5, God says:

> ²I have loved you, saith the LORD. Yet ye say, Wherein hast thou loved us? *Was* not Esau Jacob's brother? saith the LORD: yet I loved Jacob, ³And I hated Esau, and laid his mountains and his heritage waste for the dragons of the wilderness. ⁴Whereas Edom [Edom is Russia today] saith, We are impoverished [and Russia is impoverished because

of the cold and icy conditions making growing enough food to sustain themselves almost an impossible task. They do not have the ideal conditions, but we have been blessed here in the Americas], but we will return and build the desolate places; thus saith the LORD of hosts, They shall build, but I will throw down; and they shall call them, The border [border means territory] of wickedness, and, The people against whom the LORD hath indignation for ever. ⁵And your eyes shall see, and ye shall say, The LORD will be magnified from the border of Israel.

So now, we've established the players in these two wars. The bad represents those who hate God (Esau's atheistic countrymen and allies) versus our Almighty Father, the Creator of Everything.

Russia has always had their eyes on what is known as our state of Alaska today, and before long they will invade (or try to invade) this territory. Big mistake!

People need to watch current events. Russia of today is busy rebuilding themselves, even as we speak. They will become, if not already, our number one adversary, but always remember verse four where God says, "*I will throw down*"—and He will. When God says it, it leaves no room for debate! They hate God, so God hates them! (It sounds fair to me.)

It's an interesting read for you to go to your computer and pull up *Sewards Folly* and learn how Alaska was purchased. There is no doubt to me that God prearranged this acquisition so that His prophecy can come to pass exactly as it is written in God's Word.

God works in many ways, and He has His reasons and time lines. Always trust God and *never* doubt Him. Never try to second-guess Him.

God says in 1 Corinthians 15:58, "⁵⁸Therefore, my beloved brethren, be ye stedfast, unmoveable, always abounding in the work of the Lord, forasmuch as ye know that your labour is not in vain in the Lord."

Now, God is going to tell us the facts concerning how He will personally fight these wars:

¹Therefore, thou son of man, prophesy against Gog, and say, Thus saith the Lord GOD; Behold, I *am [God's holy name: I am that I am]* against thee, O Gog, the chief prince [the Russian leader] of Meshech [Moscow of today. Your Hebrew Dictionary will give you this geographical location] and Tubal (Ezekiel 39:1).

¹⁴Therefore, son of man, prophesy and say unto Gog, Thus saith the Lord GOD; In that day when my people of Israel [this is about us] dwelleth safely, shalt thou not know *it*? ¹⁵And thou shalt come from thy place out of the north parts [we are talking about Russia from the North coming down into Alaska upon us to make war] thou, and many people with thee, all of them riding upon horses [horses signifies strength, much like our horsepower in automobiles today] a great company, and a mighty army: ¹⁶And thou shalt come up against my people of Israel [that's us] as a cloud to cover the land [cloud means that it is a superhuge army]; it shall be in the latter days, and I will bring thee against my land, that the heathen [the atheistic peoples] may know me, when I shall be sanctified in thee [they'll see quickly God saying that "I am that I am, and that I am the one and only God!"] O Gog, before their eyes. ²²And I will plead against him with pestilence and with blood; and I will rain upon him, and upon his bands, and upon the many people that *are* with him, an overflowing rain, and great hailstones, fire, and brimstone [These hailstones were also recorded by God way back in the book of Joshua] (Ezekiel 28:14–16, 22).

¹¹And it came to pass, as they [our enemies] fled from before Israel [this is our forefathers] *and* were in the going down to Bethhoron, that the LORD cast down great stones [hailstones] from heaven [the clouds] upon them unto Azekah, and they died: *they were* more which died with hailstones than *they* whom the children of Israel slew with

the sword. [Our Father wants you to see here that *He* has total control over mother nature. Mother nature, if God wishes, is the most deadly weapon ever created. *Nothing can* escape the *total* destruction that these hailstones will cause. Atomic bombs cannot compete with God's mother nature (Joshua 10:11).

²¹And there fell upon men a great hail out of heaven, *every stone* about the weight of a talent [100–200 lbs.]: and men blasphemed God because of the plague of the hail; for the plague thereof was exceeding great (Revelations 16:21).

⁷So will I make my holy name known in the midst of my people Israel [the people here are you and I]; and I will not *let them* pollute my holy name any more: and the heathen shall know that I *am* the Lᴏʀᴅ, the Holy One in Israel. (Ezekiel 39:7–8).

These two massive attacks by our Father against these communistic invaders will be the largest example of God's powers that we, the people, has and will ever see, and there is no better time in history for all the doubters and unbelievers to witness such an event. (Remember Sodom and Gomorrah?)

These wars will be over within minutes; God takes care of business! He needs *no* help from us.

I do believe that the *real* and *true* Christians in this world are few and far between. *True* Christians will *not* be harmed in these two wars, but woe unto everyone else. God isn't mad at the *true* Christians but is upset with *all* of the wicked and evil, the "rudiments."

Almost all so-called Christians have differing beliefs and opinions because one preacher over here says one thing and another preacher over there says another thing, so who in the world are you to believe?

How about simply believing what God has to say? Why not seek out God's wisdom instead of man's?

Mankind makes mistakes, God doesn't!

It is imperative that all peoples of this world educate themselves in God's Word because the end of this the second earth age is rapidly coming to an end. This *is* the last generation, and you *must* believe that. Most of us who are alive today *will* witness these two major events.

How could anyone come face-to-face with God Himself and say to Him, "Sorry Father, I didn't take time to learn your word; I was too busy," or you might say, "Father, my pastor taught me all I know, and now I'm finding out that he didn't teach me truth, but instead he filled my head with lies, and I was stupid enough to go for it."

Throughout the Bible, God has warned us to be very careful with stuff we fill our minds with. Make sure that it is *truth*, not lies.

Everywhere we look, its' deception, deception, deception. God has told us, "Be not deceived," but the vast majority of the people *are* deceived. They live in deception and appear to be happy with it! How sad—how *very* sad.

Everything that a church teaches their people should align 100 percent with God's Word. It is up to *you* to verify in God's Word *all* things that you are hearing from your preacher.

Are these messages *fact* or *fiction*? You need to know! The ultimate demise of your very soul relies on your *true knowledge* of our Father's word, not some undereducated blowhard.

Believing lies can land a person in Hell to be blotted out. Surely you don't want that, do you? Of course, you don't.

Satan uses his most deadly weapon—*deception*—to win followers, and with all the awful and terrible things happening in this world today in the name of religion, it does appear that he is doing quite an excellent job. Satan truly believes that he can beat God by enticing people with his fly-away message concerning his rapture lies, and millions and millions of people are eating it up! There *is* no rapture!

Many, many people will believe that Satan, claiming to be Christ, is the "true savior." People are being taught by lying preachers, the very preachers that God has warned us about all throughout His Holy and sacred word of truth.

These lying preachers need to get their facts straight. (Maybe they *know* that they are doing Satan's work.) Could they be of Satan? (Only God knows. I say that if it quacks like a duck, it is a duck!)

People need to know how to easily tell the fake Jesus from the true Jesus. Here is how. Satan appears at the *sixth trump*, and we are still in our flesh bodies. Pinch yourself, you'll see.

The *true savior* appears at the *seventh trump*, and we are instantly, in the blink of an eye, changed back into our angelic bodies. See how easy it is to tell.

When Satan appears, he will be doing his thing for only five months, *not years*, as commonly taught. At the end of Satan's five months, our true Savior arrives, and the Millennium begins.

If your preacher is teaching these rapture lies, you need to find yourself some other place to worship (unless you enjoy being deceived).

God hates these lying preachers. I have already written of this. Go to Ezekiel 13 and read it for yourself. Do it now. Read verses twenty through twenty-three.

Then ask yourself, "Who do I believe? Do I believe in Satan or in our Heavenly Father?"

God has given us the gift of free will, so *choose wisely*.

THIS IS AN EXCITING TIME (TO LIVE)

What a time to live! Even the disciples wanted to live in *this* generation, the *last* one. Why? Because it is payback time for (1) all the people who have left God out of their everyday lives, (2) those people who have totally disregarded God's commandments, and (3) those who are doubters.

It is high time that wrong is set right!

Yes there *is* a payday, and it is just around the corner! The disciples wanted to see God's wrath come down on those who have cursed him, belittled Him, doubted Him, who couldn't care less, and those who have *not* studied to show themselves approved. God is real. God is *not* a fairy tale!

All people around the globe will see for themselves that there *is a God*—a living God, *the God of gods*, and the *only* true Supreme God. All the fakes, including fake preachers, will be put to shame and humiliation. They will be unable to spread more lies and false doctrines. Thank God!

The sad part is that the *vast* majority of all the peoples are going *away* from our Savior rather than *to* our Savior. They just move backwards!

There has never been a time in history that so many false religions have existed. There has never been a time when we have had so many lying false preachers around this world. It's astounding and sad. They are misleading those who are truly searching for truth.

Look at the Middle East and at all the unrest that we see. The bombings that result in mass murders with the killing of innocent men, women, and children are done in the name of religion. Wow! What a religion!

I too agree with the disciples. I want to personally see the evil people get their just and worthless "rewards" on Judgment Day. What a payback time that will be! We all will also get to see the final demise of the hoards of false preachers out there, and I thank God for it. (It's about time!)

How about all the crooked politicians? Have you seen any one lately? Of course! They lie to us daily! They need to be ousted now. These politicians have brought much pain upon the American people by putting heavy burdens on us all while they give themselves a much easier road to travel. It's simply pathetic! It's unfair! Yet, it continues. Where is the equality?

My hope is for the American people to rise up at the ballot box and rid ourselves of these hapless Harry Reeds, the Nancy Pelosis, the Obamas, and *all* the other ilk of like-minded screwballs. These people are a growing cancer on our society as a whole. They are extremely dangerous to our country. It's high time that we *wake up*! So go vote for the *right thing*! Don't vote left, vote right. (Fish out of the "right side of the boat," Christ says.) Socialism and communism has no place here in God's promise land.

Our children are affected in many negative areas today. It is natural for our offsprings to have a monkey-see-monkey-do frame of mind.

However the things that they see being done now is in no way like the things *we* saw when my specific generation were being raised. Ideologies are totally different in today's world. Where are the morals? Where are the *true* Christians?

We were taught respect for the elderly, we were taught not to sass our parents, and we were taught that there is a Heaven and that there is a Hell. We were taught to save our money. We were taught that our parent's parameters were never to be crossed. We were taught right from wrong. We were taught about repentance. We were taught God's Word, and we were taught how to obey His word and the importance of it. We were taught honesty.

Now we have a bunch of spoon-fed spoiled brats! Some are good, but most are bad in my opinion, and it is the fault of the parents of today plus our educational system; but the real problems with the younger generation is the fact that the parents have failed to teach them about our Lord and Savior, Jesus Christ. If the parents don't care, then their kids don't care as well. It makes sense, but it is a sad fact.

I don't think the parents know enough about *God's Holy Word* to teach them anything much anyway and therein, no doubt, lies the *real* and actual problem.

If the kids *do* have true Christian loving parents, they indeed are greatly blessed especially if they are taught to include God in the equation of their daily lives. If the kids go a little off course, don't worry, they'll return to their Christian upbringing as time goes by. They'll be fine. (God promises this.)

The main reason that I write this is that at the end of this the last generation, we will all be back with our Creator, and total discipline will be restored. At the end of this Millennium period of time, all the problems that we are having around the globe today will finally be over and done away with. (And I thank God for this.)

The Millennium is referred to and called all throughout God's Word, as you recall, the *Lord's Day*.

Christ's disciples knew that at the end of this Millennium everyone would get exactly what they had to coming to them, and that will be the most exciting event ever! No more bad stuff.

Judgment Day is common knowledge among most so-called Christians, but *it is the day of all days* that *true Christians* look forward to. You must distinguish for yourself whether you are a so-called Christian or a *real Christian*. They are as far apart, in most cases, as daylight and darkness. Perhaps you should take a personal inventory concerning your personal knowledge of God's Word. Be totally honest with yourself because your ultimate destiny is at stake here. Men's words can easily lead you astray, but God's words will not. It's essential that you know the difference about whether it's God's Words that you are following or something that some person has stated to you as being the truth. *Don't* live dangerously as most people do. Don't partake of "man's traditions." This is a serious warning from God.

Most religions out there do *not* teach you the real and complete truths of God's Word, and this is absolutely disturbing because it is detrimental concerning the ultimate demise of your soul. Don't lose your soul, it's the last and most important thing that you possess, and you should guard it carefully.

God's disciples preached their hearts out in their travels back in those days and faced many dangers along the highways and byways of that time. Their job was to spread God's Word so that it could be passed on to all future generations and, yes, they did a fantastic service for our Savior.

Just look at the perils they faced.

The disciples had no modern transportation as we have today. They had no platform of modern technology to air God's truths to the millions of people as we have today, but yet they carried on, oftentimes in dire situations, and in the end it was a job well done. (I can't help but wonder, how many of today's so-called preachers would agree to take on a responsibility like that.)

To be rid of all the idiocy in our world will have been worth the wait, and I am so very proud to be alive today.

(Yes what a time to live!)

Remember, we are all in the *last generation*, and whether you believe in God or not, all of God's prophecies *will* come to pass before *your* very eyes in this generation.

This generation began in 1948 when Israel was reestablished. It is written.

So how long is a generation? Answer: A generation, in God's Word, is 40 years, 70 years, or 120 years, or anywhere in-between at God's choosing.

You do the math!

Do you see? Time is closing in on us all. Be prepared!

(Christ said: "I have foretold you all things" and "Haven't you read?")

9

MIDDLE EAST: WE HAVE THE POWER (OVER ALL OF OUR ENEMIES)

God's power is magnificent beyond words. He passes some of His *holy power* on to us *if* He's sure that we have the works, knowledge, and faith to use them correctly.

This is old news to a "true Christian," but maybe it's new news to the many new *true* believers of God's holy Word who has recently *seen the light* and has converted to the only *truth* that exists.

Only *truth* comes from our Heavenly Father's mouth, and, sooner or later, people will realize that true *Christianity is not a religion but a reality*. Religious teachings *can* get you into trouble when it goes against our Father's true teachings, but God's truth always projects the way it is, not silly fantasies! Just facts!

For God to give us these certain powers, we must first have *true* belief and faith in every word that He says and do our best to live the life that God demands of us.

I know, and God knows, that we mess up every now and then, but through our repentance, He will wipe the slate clean, and we can move on (*if* the repentance is sincere). God always uses that *if* word because it presents us with a stipulation. He's saying to us, "I'll do this if...."

The power that is most important at this time to all *true Christians* would be to somehow gain power over Satan and his evil spirits, over all his lying coworkers, over any entity that comes against us in our lifetime here in these flesh bodies, and even have the power bestowed upon us over *all* of our enemies.

Well, I have great news. God *has* given us that power! All we have to do is *use* it in God's name.

True Christians do not need to be a doormat for anyone. We are not second-class citizens. In fact, we are the *only* first-class citizens on the face of this earth!

We take that next challenge, we don't give up to *any* challenge! We are *true* Christians! We stand for *right*.

(Now keep in mind that there is a "boatload" of difference between someone *claiming* to be a Christian and someone who *is* a *true* Christian.) You need to learn the difference.

To simply *say* that you are a Christian does not necessarily *make* you a Christian.

Talk is cheap, but actions and *works run deep*. See the difference now?

Faith without works does not count—sorry. (It's a fact!)

God says in James 2:14, 17–18, 20:

> [14]What *doth it* profit, my brethren, though a man say he hath faith, and have not works? can faith save him? [17]Even so faith, if it hath not works, is dead, being alone. [18]Yea, a man may say, Thou hast faith, and I have works: shew me thy faith without thy works, and I will shew thee my faith by my works. [20]But wilt thou know, O vain man, that faith without works is dead?

Identifying the *true* Christian is very important because God has given *us* the power to repel (to chase off) any of Satan's evil spirits that may, from time to time, come up against us. He also extended that power to include any and *all* of our enemies by using common sense.

This is a supergreat blessing! We don't have to put up with anything evil or negative.

How are we to use this power? Answer: If we pray in God's name and order any evil spirit out of your life and/or home. Evil spirits are afraid of us; they'll quickly flee!

In Luke 10:19–20, God says: "[19]Behold, I give unto you power to tread on serpents and scorpions, and over all the power of the enemy: and nothing shall by any means hurt you. [20]Notwithstanding in this rejoice not, that the spirits are subject unto you; but rather rejoice, because your names are written in heaven."

By utilizing this power to its completeness, we must anoint the entrances of our home. God us has given also to all true Christians the power of anointing, and we all should honor that God-given power by using it as often as we feel a need.

God says in James 5:14, "[14]Is any sick among you? let him call for the elders of the church; and let them pray over him, anointing him with oil in the name of the Lord."

Olive oil is *the* oil of our people, and it's the oil that God is talking about here. It isn't the oil that heals but doing things God's way *is* the key to healing. God's way is *always* the answer.

The *sick* as mentioned here can mean *the weary* or *the worn out*, and if that sick person *asks* you to anoint him, do so by simply using a little dab on your finger and touching it to the forehead while asking God to heal the person *if* it is God's will. (Remember to always anoint *in God's will*.)

My hope to you is that if there is anyone out there who truly wants to come into God's healing ways, you can now see how our Father projects His love out to us. Our Father's wish about all is for the *truly lost* to become *truly saved*.

God says in James 5:19–20, "[19]Brethren, if any of you do err from the truth, and one convert him; [20]Let him know, that he which converteth the sinner from the error of his way shall save a soul from death, and shall hide a multitude of sins."

Good works, doing things God's way wipes out a bunch of our sins. Isn't that a huge blessing!

CHRIST'S SECOND COMING

The *first* coming of Jesus Christ in the flesh took place over two thousand years ago. Why *did* Christ come? Was His one and only reason to die for our sins? Oh no, it's much more than that.

He came to select and gather twelve special men to walk the highways and byways of time and to prove to us, by His perfection, that He is our one and only key to salvation. They were chosen to spread the Gospel of Jesus Christ.

Christ would say, "Follow me." These two words are just as important for us today, and we should never ever forget them because by following Christ, we gain a much easier walk down the highway of life knowing that He will never leave us or forsake us. Why? He will never leave us or forsake us because He loves His children. His love for us is so deeply imbedded in His heart that it is impossible for us to even fathom the magnitude of it.

Through the mercy of Jesus, He performed many, many miracles by healing the sick, comforting the poor and downtrodden, and restoring sight to the blind. Christ wanted to come, in the very same flesh bodies that we have, to set an example for us to live by.

Paul, the apostle, puts it this way in Hebrews 2:9, 14:

> [9]But we see Jesus, who was made a little lower than the angels for the suffering of death, crowned with glory and honour; that he by the grace of God should taste death for every man. [14]Forasmuch then as the children are partakers of flesh and blood, he also himself likewise took part of the same; that through death he might destroy him that had the power of death, that is, the devil.

By Christ's coming, He proved to mankind that He can get the job done and get it done with perfection.

Can't you see His abounding love for us?

Christ wants us to watch, listen, and learn! So let's do it!

The excellent teachings in our Father's word is actually very plain and simple for us to follow. God's truth is to the point. He teaches that we can choose God's way or we can choose Satan's way by utilizing God's gift of free will to mankind. We have the choice to choose.

But because of the vast amount of *deception* that is being spewed out from behind the pulpits in our so-called churches in the world, what are we to believe?

If you'll remember, I have told you that *deception* is our number one enemy. Never forget that. It is Satan's lethal weapon, and he uses it very, very well. (I give him an A+ at that.)

Many, many people will tell you *emphatically* that they are Christians, but then our *real* test of *true* Christianity rests with our Father at the Great White Throne Judgment at the very end of the Lord's Day, the Millennium. No one can fool God with words. He sees all, He hears all.

Because of *deception*, I must inform you that the vast majority of mankind has already chosen Satan as their "king and savior," and what is so sad about it is they are being deceived and do not even know it. How is this possible? Well, because the so-called preachers in these so-called churches are preaching lies. These church members *think* that they are Christian but most of these people, while meaning well, are living in a world of fantasy and make-believe. Sitting in a pew and listening to nonsense does not make a person a Christian.

I'm not judging these people, but it seems to me that common sense and discernment should kick in gear at some point. How can a person sit in a pew Sunday after Sunday, year after year, believing and accepting as *fact* each and everything that is being taught (without checking out the *true* facts in God's Holy Word) is beyond my realm of thinking. It appears to me that people are living in a trance, maybe more like zombies. To *believe* lies will *not* get you to Heaven. We are living in the last generation. Everything is running fast and furious. The sands of time are running out, and I plead with you to verify, verify, and verify some more to make *sure* that you are being taught truth. Don't wait until it is one day too late.

Following "man's traditions" of lies and false dreams is a very common but ignorant thing to do in today's world of confusion.

I'm trying to teach you that true Christianity is not a religion, it is a reality. Your "religion" can very well become a stumbling block for you in your quest to make it to Heaven.

How many "religions" are there in this world? (Answer: A bunch.) They are not many if any teaching God's truth because *all* of these "religions" teach something different. They are all convinced that their way is the best way.

But wait, how about God's way? Who in this world is teaching us God's way? Well, *God* is—*duh*—He sent us a book of instructions. It's called the Bible. Have you read it with understanding?

I have told you earlier in these writings about the tools that you'll need to use to dig out God's *true* teachings on your own. People need to allow God to be their one and only preacher; therefore, you can be certain that you are learning truth as God has intended from the beginning. God wants us to study, to show ourselves approved. Listening to falsehoods is *not* studying.

Now, on to the events that are happening now that spell out a timetable for our Father's second return to us His children.

Christ's *first* return is called the *first advent*. Christ's second return is called the *second advent*.

In Christ's *first advent*, He came here to earth to be *crucified*, thus setting the stage for us to have something called *repentance*. His Crucifixion showed His children that His love for us is so strong that He would lay down His life so that we could have redemption through repentance. Christ was our "blood sacrifice" for one and all times.

At death on the cross (a Roman punishment of the time), He proved to us that He has the power to defeat death (that is to say, Satan). He also wanted to show us that there *is* a God.

The prophecy concerning Christ's crucifixion was penned by David in Psalms 22. This prophecy was written one thousand years before the Crucifixion took place. It even states that the men were gambling for His robe at the foot of the cross, and while on that cross, Christ quoted that entire twenty second chapter of Psalms. He wanted for us to know that His prophecies come true even unto the slightest detail.

Christ's second coming is drawing near; we don't know the exact time, but He has showed us the *season* so that we can stay alert to the events taking place around the world. These events will consummate His second advent. The events are well recorded in God's Word. Israel is our barometer to watch. Follow the events that are happening there very, very closely. People are crying, "Peace, peace," but there is no peace.

God is allowing Satan's evil spiritual influence upon all peoples of the earth. God is allowing Satan's spirit to infest *every single entity* of our world. He is allowed to morally corrupt even the churches (religions), our entire money system (through usury), our governmental systems, and our educational systems, and I must add that he has become very successful at doing his job.

These four systems are referred to as Satan's "Four Hidden Dynasties" or four hidden powers. And we have already discussed these four dynasties in the previous chapter. It is useful to go back and read that again to absorb even more.

Christ's *first* coming involved riding on a lowly ass to be crucified for our sins and it was a *job well done*. But upon Christ's *second* coming, He'll be riding a powerful white steed, and with Him will be a rod of iron to be used for the corrections of His children. For a while there will be no more "Mr. Nice Guy." At His appearance, *every* knee shall bow (kneel before Him), and I mean *every* knee. Every one kneels—the atheists, the agnostics, the homosexuals, the druggies, the rapists, the murderers, the good, the bad, the ugly, the pretty, and so forth. (You get the point.)

At that *second* coming, people will know without a doubt that there *is* a God. There will be no more doubters. They'll see with their own eyes the Father of us all. His majestic beauty will be breathtaking! Awesomeness will abound! Words cannot describe it.

We *all* need to follow God's Words of instructions as best as we possibly can; but always remember radical thinking is *out*, God's personal word to us is *in*!

I want to hear God say to me, "A job well done my son." I sincerely hope that He'll say these words to many, many, many of us.

Don't you? Of course you do!

NEVER FORGET
THESE TWELVE TRUE FACTS

The primary purpose for writing this book is an attempt to reach out to the people by teaching them, straight from God's Word, the following absolute facts that are *not* covered in other religious writings of today.

In this book,

I dismiss all organized religions because God does!

I dismiss all of man's false teachings and doctrine because God does!

I dismiss all denominations because God does!

I dismiss all the false teachings that there is but *one* God.

There is only one *true God* (with a capital *G*) and there is another *god* (with a lower case *g*) and his name is Satan who *calls himself* the only "true god." (Are you deceived?)

I dismiss all man's religious traditions (which are vain and empty) because God does!

I dismiss all misinformed and lying so-called preachers, pastors, or any other so-called church leaders who teach everything but God's actual truth, because God does!

In this book, you will learn straight from God the following twelve facts that a person's destiny rests:

1. How we, the people, got here and where we are headed.
2. That this *is* the last generation of *all* flesh.
3. How our existence ends.
4. What our true purpose is for being here.
5. That we have two bodies, and they both look the same.
6. That God dishes out curses as well as blessings.
7. How to achieve *true* salvation instead of fake salvation.
8. That God is our *next of kin.*
9. About dire warnings from God Himself to all of His children throughout the world.
10. That there is truly a Judgment Day coming, and that it is closer than one may think.
11. That reading the Bible (the King James Version only) is like listening or reading tomorrow's news.
12. You'll learn *one very profound statement* from God saying that we must believe in Him and have *true faith* in Him because He tells us:

"I CANNOT LIE."

None of God's words are open for debate. God's Word is absolute!

THE FOREVER MIDDLE EAST UNREST (WHY THE MANY LANGUAGES WERE FORMED)

Do you recall that I quoted to you God's Scripture where he said, "I have foretold you all things?" (Here is how and why the languages we use today began.)

We can go back to Genesis, written some 4000–5000 Bc, and learn *why* we have today (and always have had) confusion in the Middle Eastern countries.

Confusion among the peoples there began with the attempted building of the Tower of Babel, near where Baghdad, Iraq is located today. Even the word *Babel* means confusion.

At the time of this construction, the peoples of the earth spoke but one language, *one speech* as recorded in Genesis 11:1–9. (Take a moment to read it yourself.)

> ¹And the whole earth was of one language, and of one speech. ²And it came to pass, as they journeyed from the east, that they found a plain in the land of Shinar; and they dwelt there. ³And they said one to another, Go to, let us make brick, and burn them throughly. And they had brick for stone, and slime had they for morter. ⁴And they said, Go to, let us build us a city and a tower, whose top *may reach* unto heaven; and let us make us a name, lest we be scattered abroad upon the face of the whole earth. ⁵And the LORD came down to see the city and the tower, which the children of men builded. ⁶And the LORD said, Behold, the people *is* one, and they have all one language; and this they begin to do: and now nothing will be restrained from them, which they have imagined to do. ⁷Go to, let us go down, and there confound their language, that they may not understand one another's speech. ⁸So the LORD scattered them abroad from thence upon the face of all the earth: and they left off to build the city. ⁹Therefore is

the name of it called Babel; because the LORD did there confound the language of all the earth: and from thence did the LORD scatter them abroad upon the face of all the earth.

Now this tower was built to save them in case another flood, like Noah's, should occur. The tower would be their "true salvation" or, you could say, their "stairway to heaven."

This, the construction of this so-called *tower of salvation*, was a very stupid thing they were doing because, as we all know (or should know), salvation must go through God, not some tower or tall building. (This is an excellent example to prove that *true salvation* can only come from God.)

The Tower of Babel *fell*, killing a few dozen of the workers. (The falling of the tower represents to us that if we try to find any other way to the safety of salvation except through our *true Father*, it will not stand—it *will* fall.)

God was watching all of this (just as He watches *this* day) and put upon them a great confusion. God confounded their language, creating mass confusion among the people because they could in no way understand what one person was saying to another. (Here began God's creation of the languages of today.)

Mass confusion is a terrible punishment that God put on mankind, and it happened in the very geographical location that all the horrible uprisings, killings, people blowing up each other, and so forth are happening this very day.

Down through history, in the name of religion, the fighting has continued and it always will. (Don't worry because God is in control—*total control.*)

We, here in this country, have absolutely wasted the lives of thousands of our warriors over there, and what good came of it? None!

We could fight over there for a thousand years and it still would have no effect on those Godless peoples. They do not want a peaceful democracy.

If our so-called leaders of this country were *true* Christians, they would have realized that God is in control, and there is no army (or all armies in the world) that can change those people. (Why? They live in confusion!)

I believe that we should have never put our men and women in harm's way over there because of the vast confusion that exists (and always will).

Only God can bring peace there, and He will do it in *His* own appointed time, not our appointed time.

The Middle East is not the only place that confusion reigns. We too are a confused and confounded nation. (Look at the hundreds of thousands of people that met their fate right here in America in our *own* civil war.)

We are also a confused nation when it comes down to the only true path to *salvation*. All of our so-called religions here have, according to them, worked out their own "paths" to achieve salvation, and some of their beliefs are just as radical as those nuts over there in those countries.

An atheist is an atheist no matter where he lives on earth.

Socialism and communism is still socialism and communism no matter where it abides on this earth.

All the evilness and deceit will cease at the appearance of our one and only Father on high, and I pray, in His will, that it will be soon. Enough is enough! Amen. (Amen means *there's no more to be said.*)

What did we learn other than the creation of languages? Answer: There is only *one way* to save ourselves from Hell and that is *God's way*!

WANT TO BE RICH?
(AN INVESTMENT MUST)

If you want to be rich by the time you die, or actually long before you die, there is only one investment that you can make that pays the dividends that *this* investment will make you, and that dividend will be paid directly to you tax-free.

Does this sound too good to be true? Well, it *is* true! *All* of the dividends are absolutely *tax-free*, and on top of that, you have for certain *no risk* involved concerning this important investment.

All that you'll have to invest is your time. No money is involved in purchasing this, the *greatest of all* returns. It's a win–win investment. No investor has *ever* lost.

The investment concerns the destiny of your very *soul*, and how you go about nourishing it.

The more you feed it, the larger the dividend! It's just that simple. So who wouldn't want to make an investment like that?

The time that you spend feeding your soul with God's truth is invaluable. The untrue teachings will pay you nothing but a ticket to Hell if you believe in them. (I'm writing this book for you in hopes that you will take the lessons seriously, which I've laid out in the prayerful hope that you'll personally respond in a positive way not to me, but to our Father in Heaven.)

The dollars, the gold, the silver, and all the precious gems that exist in the world are worth absolutely *nothing* at the very second that you die. Your efforts to gain these assets were all for naught. All of a sudden, they are worthless! Totally worthless—to *you*, that is!

There is nothing wrong with having riches, assuming they are not ill-gotten gains, but to allow no-set-aside time to study God's Word is, in itself, a very, very bad thing to do. Your return will be nil.

A person should always put God first. Then secondly, you can pursue your dreams, being honest, and have an abundance of

God's blessings. Whatever you do, "if it's honest, it's honorable," and *always* adhere to that quote.

I personally have done my absolute best to stick with those words, and I know that it will pay me *big-time* dividends, not necessarily in worldly riches; but I fully expect a bountiful payday when I meet my loving Father because I have invested wisely in countless hours of learning the true value of the *Heavenly dividends* that I will receive on Judgment Day.

Now let's talk seriously about this. Here are the two facts that you must know:

1. It is *never* too late to join the "investment club."

2. You'll be paid the very same dividends if you join at ten years old or one hundred years old. It's true. The late investors get the same reward. (For that matter, there are no age restrictions involved at all.) It's all up to you, but let me warn you about something that is of extreme importance, and that is—you *can* wait "one day too late." (And that could be lethal!) To get no return on your life is a very sad thing.

Allow me to quote to you God's *truth* concerning the fact that it is *never too late to get to work*:

In Matthew 20:1–16, God says:

> [1]For the kingdom of heaven is like unto a man that is an householder, which went out early in the morning to hire labourers into his vineyard. [2]And when he had agreed with the labourers for a penny a day, he sent them into his vineyard. [3]And he went out about the third hour, and saw others standing idle in the marketplace, [4]And said unto them; Go ye also into the vineyard, and whatsoever is right I will give you. And they went their way. [5]Again he went out about the sixth and ninth hour, and did likewise. [6]And about the eleventh hour he went out, and found others standing idle, and saith unto them, Why stand ye here all the day idle? [7]They say unto him, Because no man hath hired us. He saith unto them, Go ye also into the vineyard; and whatsoever is right, that shall ye receive.

[8]So when even was come, the lord of the vineyard saith unto his steward, Call the labourers, and give them their hire, beginning from the last unto the first. [9]And when they came that were hired about the eleventh hour, they received every man a penny. [10]But when the first came, they supposed that they should have received more; and they likewise received every man a penny. [11]And when they had received it, they murmured against the goodman of the house, [12]Saying, These last have wrought but one hour, and thou hast made them equal unto us, which have borne the burden and heat of the day. [13]But he answered one of them, and said, Friend, I do thee no wrong: didst not thou agree with me for a penny? [14]Take that thine is, and go thy way: I will give unto this last, even as unto thee. [15]Is it not lawful for me to do what I will with mine own? Is thine eye evil, because I am good? [16]So the last shall be first, and the first last: for many be called, but few chosen.

Okay. We've learned a lot here! Everyone gets the same pay! It doesn't matter if we are early or late getting into God's Word because God is fair. This parable is of the utmost importance for you to never forget. (Just don't wait until it is that "one day too late.") Our Father loves us dearly and sincerely, and He wants you to join the *club of winners*.

So do it. Do it now. On payday, you will truly rejoice!

You'll be very, very happy that you joined the club.

10

A SALUTE TO SHEPHERD'S CHAPEL
(AN UPDATE)

Arnold Murray passed away on February 12, 2014, but Shepherd's Chapel will continue airing his lectures.

So you can still listen and learn. This is excellent advice *if* you truly want to learn God's Words of truth from a *tried and true* Christian scholar.

There are a lot of people out there who claim to be "scholars" but, believe me, it's a lie. They aren't. (They are simply would-bes.)

A true scholar who knew the manuscripts inside and out and possessed the special *gift of charisma* so that he could present God's Word in a way that one can easily understand in an exciting manner, making a person eager to learn more and more and more.

Arnold Murray had it all.

His passing leaves an empty feeling in my heart.

He *is* my personal mentor.

I will forever be indebted to Shepherds Chapel. It has been a soul-saving experience for me to have an opportunity to be taught "how to learn" and have the tools to obtain to verify the so-called teachings of man to see if the information being preached to everyone is really *truth* or simply "man's traditions."

To learn God's Word by being taught chapter by chapter and line by line and book by book is absolutely the *only* way—I repeat—the *only* manner to truly get the full picture and intended message that God wants us to know and understand.

To possess the charisma that Arnold Murray, the pastor, had is a mighty blessing to him directly from our Heavenly Father, and although I did not know him personally, I do know that He was so thankful of this *special blessing* that was bestowed upon him. He used it wisely.

For all of you out there, I will offer you a challenge: If you'll find him on your local station (his sermons will continue to be broadcasted nearly around-the-clock) and if you will listen to these teachings, straight from God's Holy Word, with the true meanings being explained, you *will* be *hooked on truth*—and always remember, "Truth will set you free!" It truly will!

Set aside a particular hour of the day to learn and do not miss any of his lectures. He picks up where he left off in the previous lecture.

Shepherds Chapel has a great format. Thirty minutes of lectures and thirty minutes of questions and answers sent in by the listeners on a daily basis. The pastor always allows the scriptures to give you the answers.

I've been through the King James Version Bible many times in the past thirty years, and I assure you that there is no better place to learn in this day and time. Arnold Murray never begged you for money either. His vocation was to teach God's Word. It was his mission.

They do not have telethons or put on a show of some sort or any other nonsense. They teach from a sitting position behind a desk, just the same as when we were in school.

Now I must make this statement: Shepherds Chapel has *not* endorsed this book or any statement that I have written, nor have

I requested an endorsement from them, and I do not intend to. (But one would be welcomed!)

However, I do believe that I have my Father's endorsement. I *know* I do!

I wrote this book for only *one purpose* and that was to write it in such a way that anyone can understand without using those "confusing big words." My hopes are that if just one person out there can be reached and convinced to become a *true* Christian and to become eager to learn God's true word, then I know that God, our Heavenly Father, will consider this writing a best seller!

I pray that God will bless this book, *if* it is His will.

Amen.

POLITICIANS AND THE MEDIA
(THE ARENA OF COMEDY)

Here is how I see things. If I had God's power, I would judge these people using these words:

Hillary Clinton

"I stand by my man," she once said on national TV concerning her husbands "sex play" allegations. Where are *your* morals? She's all about *ego*, nothing else. If she runs for president, ignore her. She's not worth listening to. A waste of time. *Go away!*

Bill Clinton

You degraded the highest office in our land. You and your wife deserve each other. You *both* are liars and *ego*-maniacs. People out there don't think of you as highly as you think they do! *Go Away!*

Barrack Obama

You should have never been elected to the office that you hold. You too are a liar. Everyone knows that. You need to crawl back into the hole you came out. You've created a mess. You are also an *ego*-maniac. I find you and your ilk worthless and of no value. *Go away!*

Joe Biden

You need to retire. Like your boss, you act like an idiot. You two also deserve each other. Get out! *Go away!*

Michelle Obama

You, in my opinion, are a waste of our money. You too need to go back to wherever you came from. You are worthless as well. Multimillion dollar vacations? Get real! *Go away!*

George Bush

When you began bailing out the too-big-to-fail companies, I lost confidence in you. You were raised privileged. I voted for you twice though. You also wasted tons of taxpayers' money traveling back and forth to your ranch. You live in a "different world." Live in it. Thanks for staying quiet the past few years. Now, *go away!*

Bill O'Reilly

Stick to the news. Killing Jesus was inaccurate. You say that the malefactor on the cross next to Jesus "can't be verified." Oh, really?

What Bible are *you* reading? Whoever aided you in writing that book was not a bible scholar. A lot of people *claim* to be, but they're not. Leave God's *truth* to someone else who can read the manuscripts! For now, *you may stay.*

Ted Cruz

Should be the next president, but he must produce on his promises concerning fixing the problems and doing it quickly. *Action*, not hot air, is the word of the day! Let's elect *him.*

Out With the Old–In With the New!

All broadcast television networks (ABC, NBC, CBS, and CNBC, as well as CNN) are left-wing liberal stations; and the people of our nation should never listen to their nonexisting "truth" messages! Never!

Being liberal, they are *with* the current regime. They too report lies. They slant the truth, and that is bad. God hates it. The people hate it! That's why you have low ratings!

Does anyone out there *want* to listen to newscasters who muddy the waters with less than truth? I think not!

So folks, tune them out! They are deceitful!

They do *not* report in a full and honest method. So they *must* not be of God, but of Satan instead. You think?

Beware!

This is a dire warning from God to you! God hates liars!

Never tune in to half-truths! (That's the main thing that is wrong in this nation.)

Always seek out the truth! On TV *or* church.

12

HIGHWAY OF LIFE

The "Highway of Life" is truth, truth from God's true Word. There is nothing complex about it; it's the way it is. It's reality. God's Word is always reality!

The moment that we are born, we begin our trip down the "Highway of Life." Everyone walks this highway, and it begins as an embryo. If a person dies as an embryo, he/she will immediately pass to the "Y" at the end of the "Highway of Life." If one is 18 years old, 35 years old or even a hundred years old, they immediately advance to the "Y" on the "Highway of Life". The "Y" is the ultimate end of the "Highway of Life" for everyone who has ever lived; past and present.

Death of the flesh is a fact of life.

When we die, we instantly step into our original spiritual bodies and depending on how we lived our lives here in the flesh will determine whether we are classified with a mortal or an immortal spiritual body.

A mortal body means that the person is liable to die when judged by God, at the end of the millennium at the Great White Throne Judgment.

An immortal body means that by ones good work and faith, he is blessed with deathlessness; which means that he "made the cut."

So, with the graphic that is shown with this explanation, you see that when you reach that "Y", we will all meet someone there, appointed by God, to point the people that arrived with a mortal body to the left side and the immortal bodies to the right side.

(You must keep in mind that because God gave us the gift of free will, you had total control of your destiny. So, if you end up on the bad side, you only have yourself to blame. God tells us to study to show ourselves approved. Listening to lying preachers and believing in what they say, can cause you to lose your very soul in Hell. Don't blame God because it is you who made all the wrong choices. You are the captain of your ship!)

Now, between the left side and the right side is a gulf (or chasm) whereby there can be no crossing from one side to the other. In Luke, Chapter 16, God gives us Lazarus and the rich man as a perfect example of these two sides, as well as the gulf. (You can read it for yourself.)

I go to great lengths to warn people to get their business straight with our one and only Heavenly Father because we are all only one heart-beat away from this reality to unfold before our very own eyes.

God doesn't tell us things to amuse us or entertain us. God is very real and this "Highway of Life" that we are traveling on is real. God's Word is absolute leaving absolutely no room for debate! Never doubt one word of God's Words of absolute truth.

Never put the destiny of your soul in any flesh man's hands. Don't be a fool!
Amen

Highway of Life

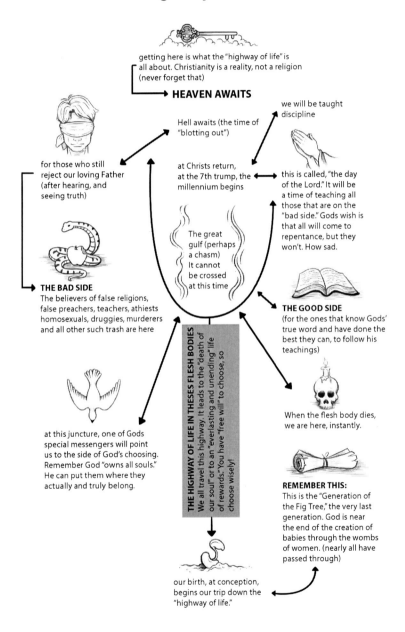

getting here is what the "highway of life" is all about. Christianity is a reality, not a religion (never forget that)

HEAVEN AWAITS

we will be taught discipline

Hell awaits (the time of "blotting out")

for those who still reject our loving Father (after hearing, and seeing truth)

at Christs return, at the 7th trump, the millennium begins

this is called, "the day of the Lord." It will be a time of teaching all those that are on the "bad side." Gods wish is that all will come to repentance, but they won't. How sad.

The great gulf (perhaps a chasm) It cannot be crossed at this time

THE BAD SIDE
The believers of false religions, false preachers, teachers, athiests homosexuals, druggies, murderers and all other such trash are here

THE GOOD SIDE
(for the ones that know Gods' true word and have done the best they can, to follow his teachings)

When the flesh body dies, we are here, instantly.

THE HIGHWAY OF LIFE IN THESES FLESH BODIES
We all travel this highway. It leads to the "death of our soul" or to an "everlasting and unending" life of rewards. You have "free will" to choose, so choose wisely!

at this juncture, one of Gods special messengers will point us to the side of God's choosing. Remember God "owns all souls." He can put them where they actually and truly belong.

REMEMBER THIS:
This is the "Generation of the Fig Tree," the very last generation. God is near the end of the creation of babies through the wombs of women. (nearly all have passed through)

our birth, at conception, begins our trip down the "highway of life."

e|LIVE

---

listen|imagine|view|experience